AF334289

This exhibition is sponsored by Exxon Corporation
with the support of the Visual Arts Board,
Australia Council

AUSTRALIAN VISIONS:

1984 EXXON

INTERNATIONAL EXHIBITION

by Diane Waldman

Solomon R. Guggenheim Museum, New York

Published by
The Solomon R. Guggenheim Foundation, New York, 1984
ISBN: 0-89207-048-x

Library of Congress Cataloging in Publication Data

Waldman, Diane.
  Australian visions.

  "This exhibition is sponsored by Exxon Corporation
with the support of the Visual Arts Board, Australia Council."
  1. Art, Australian—Exhibitions.   2. Art, Modern—
20th century—Australia—Exhibitions.   I. Solomon
R. Guggenheim Museum.   II. Exxon Corporation.
III. Australia Council.   Visual Arts Board.
IV. Title.

N7400.2.W34 1984   709′.94′07401471   84-13914
ISBN 0-89207-048-X

LENDERS TO THE EXHIBITION

Naomi Cass

Michael Darling

Mrs. E. Gregory

Bill Henson

Mandy Martin

Evi Robinson

Vivienne Sharpe

Janice and Greg Taylor

M. R. Tomkins

The University of Melbourne

John S. Walton

Art Gallery of South Australia, Adelaide

National Gallery of Victoria, Melbourne

Riddoch Art Gallery, Mount Gambier, Australia

Art Projects, Melbourne

Mori Gallery, Sydney

Roslyn Oxley9, Sydney

Pinacotheca, Melbourne

Powell Street Gallery, Melbourne

Studio d'Arte Cannaviello, Milan

TABLE OF CONTENTS

PREFACE AND ACKNOWLEDGEMENTS

Like Britain in 1980 and Italy in 1982, Australia is in 1984 the source for the *Exxon International Exhibition,* for which Diane Waldman, the Guggenheim Museum's Deputy Director, remains fully responsible.

Certain characteristics and certain largely unresolved issues recur in young talent shows drawn from abroad. Among these are the overlapping in an artist's contribution of purely personal expression and the implied responsibility for representing national identity. Inevitably, artists speak for themselves while at the same time carrying upon their shoulders, willingly, deliberately or not, a share of that collective identity that is the mark of particular ethnic and cultural origins. This exhibition and the accompanying catalogue that offers its rationalization provide a case in point with respect to Australia.

Related to these issues are the simultaneous perceptions of a regional, national and continental personality, perceptions gained from a reading of pictorial and plastic signs that have the capacity to project it. The different meanings arrived at within and without a particular geo-cultural area, as well as the autonomy and uniqueness of each context, provide us with points of departure for fairly complex speculation.

Finally, the artist's simultaneous response to the stimuli of life and art is a recurrent factor that, in terms of this selection of current Australian art, creates tensions that are inseparable from the contents of individual works and those of the show as a whole. Here, as everywhere, a creative process insufficiently oxygenated by life will thin the substance of art to the point of extinction, while, on the other hand, form-language steeped in issues remains threatened by dissolution in life itself. The difficulty inherent in a balancing act that effectively precludes both these fatalities is not one from which contemporary Australian artists can be exempted.

The testing of such generalities and their application to particular contemporary situations is the underlying purpose of the *Exxon International Exhibitions.* The Guggenheim and its public thus incur a debt to the participating artists, to the curator of the exhibition and the assisting staff, to the lenders and the sponsors, through whose aid and commitment such projects can be realized. This year the Visual Arts Board, Australia Council, has contributed its support along with that of Exxon Corporation, whose generous financing of this program over a period of many years has resulted in ever increasing tangible benefits.

Thomas M. Messer, *Director*
The Solomon R. Guggenheim Foundation

This exhibition was realized with the assistance and co-operation of many individuals. I am especially grateful to members of the Visual Arts Board, Australia Council, in particular Ann Lewis, former Chairman, for inviting me to Australia to become familiar with contemporary art there and also for her support of this project, and Nick Waterlow, former Director, for his continuing and helpful participation in every phase of the undertaking. I am also deeply indebted to Betty Churcher, Chairperson, and Ross Wolfe, Director, of the Visual Arts Board for their essential contributions. Staff of the Visual Arts Board, notably Seva Frangos, Project Officer, as well as Janet Parfenovics, Consultant, Australian and International Exhibition Management, were also extremely helpful. Visual Arts Board Members, among them Lesley Dumbrell and Margriet Bonnin are also owed gratitude for their assistance. Among the numerous individuals who offered advice and help I wish to single out for special acknowledgement William Wright, Assistant Director of the Art Gallery of New South Wales, Sydney; Ron Radford, Curator of Paintings, and Alison Carroll, Curator of Prints and Drawings, The Art Gallery of South Australia, Adelaide; Robert Lindsay, Curator of Contemporary Australian Painting, National Gallery of Victoria, Melbourne; Daniel Thomas, Senior Curator, Australian Art, Australian National Gallery, Canberra; Suzanne Davies, Vice President and Chairperson of the Print Council of Australia; and Hugh Campbell, Reference Librarian of the Australian Information Service, New York. Sincere thanks are extended to the many gallery dealers who were extremely helpful, including Christine Abrahams, Stephen Mori, Roslyn Oxley, Bruce Pollard and Pauline Wrobel.

I would particularly like to thank Guggenheim Museum staff members for their diligent efforts on behalf of the exhibition and catalogue. Among those who have been centrally involved are Susan Taylor, former Curatorial Coordinator, Susan Hapgood, Curatorial Assistant, both of whom worked closely and enthusiastically with me on all aspects of the project; Carol Fuerstein, Editor, for her insightful editing of the catalogue; and her assistant Diana Murphy for her meticulous collaboration; Stephanie Stitt, Registrar's Coordinator, and Riquita Stoutzker for their help.

My special gratitude is warmly expressed to the lenders whose generosity has made the presentation possible. Finally I would like to thank the artists themselves, who have made this exhibition a very pleasant and rewarding experience for me.

D.W.

FOREWORD

When Diane Waldman, the Deputy Director of the Guggenheim Museum, visited Australia for the first time in October 1983 as a guest of the Visual Arts Board it was very much a voyage of discovery. On that occasion she spent many hours visiting artists' studios, their galleries, talking with artists and their dealers — drawing together in her mind the many disparate strands and forming, in a very short time, an astute opinion about what was interesting and new in the art of an emerging generation.

Of course, it is never possible to represent the art of a country as large and as diverse as Australia with the work of eight artists, and in making her selection Diane Waldman has wisely relied on her instincts, backed by many years of professional experience. What links the works of the artists who were finally selected is an energy and direction that points to a discernible Australian quality— of color, of immediacy, even a rawness that relates to the nature of this country and the media — a hungry urban culture to which these artists belong.

This exhibition of Australian art at the Solomon R. Guggenheim Museum is the culmination of over a century of sporadic cultural exchange between the United States of America and Australia. Australian painting was first represented in 1866 at the Intercolonial Exhibition held in Chicago; a larger selection of Australian art was included in an international exhibition in 1975 in Philadelphia. In 1930 the Roerich Museum in New York paid the costs for an exhibition of one hundred Australian pictures, and in 1952 in Pittsburgh the Carnegie International Exhibition included works by four Australian artists.

The traffic in art between America and Australia seems, however, to have been one way, until the tide was completely turned by the important and influential *Two Decades of American Painting*, which was organized by The Museum of Modern Art in New York and shown in five cities: Tokyo, Kyoto, New Delhi, Melbourne and Sydney, between 1966 and 1967. This exhibition had a powerful effect on the Australian community and exerted a wide influence on Australian artists, especially young painters who saw for the first time the original works of major American painters of the fifties and sixties.

We in Australia are, therefore, indebted to Exxon Corporation whose innovative policy of art patronage has made this exhibition of Australian artists possible, enlarging the dialogue between our two countries.

We are also delighted to be associated with the Guggenheim Museum and are especially indebted to Diane Waldman for the care and commitment that she has brought to the selection of work and for the part she played in promoting and developing the idea of the exhibition.

Finally, we wish to pay special tribute to the artists whose participation has made this exhibition possible.

Betty Churcher, *Chairperson*
Visual Arts Board, Australia Council

IMPRESSIONS OF AUSTRALIA

by Diane Waldman

For the first-time visitor to Australia the initial impression is the overwhelming presence of the land. The vast open terrain, although tamed in the cities, is unruly in the bush and the outback, and the feeling of it is all-pervasive. So too is the immense sky which sits low on the horizon and provides a spectacular and ever changing panorama. The lush, fertile Pacific coast and the awesome rich red desert, the heat and the intensity of the light which enhances even the whitest white, the most brilliant purple or yellow, the graceful plumed birds, the ungainly, winsome animals, the eucalyptus and the ghost gum trees impress themselves indelibly on the senses in a continent full of dramatic and unexpected contrasts.

Australia has often been described as the "last frontier" and, indeed, the challenge and promise it offers lends credence to that appellation. For Europeans and Americans, Australia today still represents the romantic ideal, the dream of the paradise regained that Erasmus Darwin responded to when he first sailed into Botany Bay in 1789:

Where Sydney Cove her lucid bosom swells,
Courts her young navies, and the storm repels;
High on a rock amid the troubled air
HOPE stood sublime, and wav'd her golden hair.... [1]

Whereas aboriginal Australia is thought to have been settled some 40,000 years ago, European Australia was based upon a series of convict settlements founded in the eighteenth century. When, on January 18, 1788, a fleet of eleven ships commanded by Captain Arthur Phillip, who became the first Governor of the colony of New South Wales, reached Botany Bay over 700 of those on board were convicts. By 1840 nearly 100,000 convicts had been sent from Britain to the mainland of Australia. Although free settlers brought the population to 400,000 in 1850, convicts were transported to Tasmania until 1853 and to Western Australia from 1850 to 1856 to compensate for a serious shortage of labor.[2] The continent consisted of territories that were granted independence individually at various times; only in 1901 were the colonies federated as states to become the Commonwealth of Australia.

Despite these grim, hard beginnings, Australia became a prosperous land, developing a wool industry and a farm economy. It became as well a pioneer in social reform—national suffrage for women was achieved with federation

in 1901 — and a society whose pioneer stock, largely English and Irish, has been strengthened and enriched by an influx of Europeans of other origins and Asians. Although Australia will shortly celebrate its two hundredth anniversary, it remains a nation that came into being in the postindustrial era. A land mass just slightly smaller than our own, Australia is populated by only about fifteen million people. It is thus still very much a nation that is becoming — in its political, economic, social and cultural identity. It is this sense of becoming, of newness, of raw energy and vitality that infuses the land, the people and the art.

From its beginnings, Australia had much in common with the United States. Both were peopled largely by outcasts from Europe; as pioneers in a new land their lives were harrowing struggles for survival. They had in common traditions determined, at least in part, by their origins as British colonies. And both regarded and recorded their new landscapes with a mixture of awe and curiosity. Although Australia produced no equivalent of the Hudson River School, which emerged here in the 1820s, the German-born Eugene von Guérard, who settled in Australia in the early 1850s, reveals affinities with American nineteenth-century romantic landscape painters. Like many of the artists of the Hudson River School, von Guérard studied at the Düsseldorf Academy in Germany. Like them, he presents in his work both the majesty of nature and the fury of its forces. Although von Guérard long enjoyed acclaim in Australia, his art fell out of favor there during his lifetime. A form of naturalistic plein-air painting, similar to that of the Barbizon School popular in France, soon became the leading fashion in Australia during the late nineteenth century. However, von Guérard and other nineteenth-century figures left a meaningful legacy in initiating a landscape tradition that has prevailed throughout much of Australia's brief art-history. To be sure, that tradition was interrupted during the 1950s, 1960s and 1970s when painters, with few exceptions, looked to Europe and particularly to America for artistic models.

Despite forays into abstraction during the postwar era, little in modern Australian art rivals the sophisticated inventions of such avant-garde Americans of the early twentieth century as Arthur Dove, Georgia O'Keeffe, Stanton Macdonald-Wright or Patrick Henry Bruce. More important, Australian artists have never approached the profundity of the American committment to abstraction, as expressed by Jackson Pollock, Mark Rothko, Barnett Newman, Clyfford Still and other masters of the New York School. Yet Australians have made a unique contribution by developing an art inspired by the landscape and the figure which could have remained a merely regional idiom — as it did in the United States between the two world wars — into an authentic and powerful pictorial style.

Australia's artistic coming of age has resulted from an acknowledgement of the continent's isolation from the Western hemisphere. The isolation that in the past has engendered a deep sense of insecurity today gives rise to a growing recognition on the part of many Australians that they have a special role to play in the world. Thus, the current resurgence of figurative and landscape painting in Australia can be attributed to a new awareness of and pride in a native tradition rather than to the influence from abroad of Neo-Expressionism. Many younger artists working today have turned for inspiration to exemplary figures who came to prominence in the 1940s, such as Sidney Nolan, Albert Tucker, Arthur Boyd and John Perceval and to more recent painters such as Jan Senbergs. By revivifying their traditions, the younger Australians are able to make an original contribution to the ongoing international dialogue on art, an unheralded, singleminded contribution that is marked by immediacy and a sense of promise.

Australian art in the 1970s, prior to this resurgence, was very much like the art in major centers throughout Europe and the United States: conceptual art, video and performance predominated where painting and sculpture had previously held sway. Although little of lasting value emerged during the decade, Australian art of those years already was informed by special qualities that set it apart and lent it credibility. The subtleties and nuances, the emotional distancing of an art form that is about art — the predominant international expression of the 1970s — were absent from Australian work of that period. Instead, there was a brooding, introspective mood, a sense of urgency and drama and an intense, hothouse palette — hallmarks of much of the very different art of the 1980s in Australia.

We see in the young Australian art of today a directness, a powerful emotive sensibility that finds expression in an intense pathos or humor, a sense of melodrama, a raw energy, a rude sense of color and form and finally an awkwardness that is both uncomfortable and reassuring in its vitality and affirmation of feeling. Recent Australian art is disquieting because, like Australia itself, it directly confronts our consciousness. It refuses to be polite and quiet. It refuses to draw upon pop imagery we can consume and forget like supermarket products. Art in Australia, because it is ungainly and demanding, does not conform to our expectations of a seemly art. It asks of us rather than simply gives to us. To this extent it is unyielding and unsympathetic and distinct from the humanist landscape and portrait painting that has evolved since the Renaissance. It also stands outside the tradition of social realism in that it speaks more intensely of individual inner feelings than of the issues of the day. The paintings of Peter Booth, Dale Frank, Mandy Martin, Jan Murray, Susan Norrie, Vivienne Shark LeWitt, the photographs of Bill Henson, the installations of John Nixon are deeply, even obsessively autobiographical in nature yet they are also meaningful in what they say about Australia and about the state of art today.

Australia today is a curious amalgam, a postindustrial society superimposed upon a wilderness. It is poised close to Asia but still rooted in European tradition. It benefits from its distance from the West in its independence but suffers from the absence of first-hand information. Change is swift yet many are wary of moving too quickly into the future. Australians suffer from a certain collective neurosis based upon their isolation and their love, fear and dread of the land. Now more frequently than before, critics of the arts are questioning Australia's cultural identity.

Curiously, this visitor found that the artists themselves are relatively undisturbed by this sense of dilemma. They welcome the many visitors' increasing curiosity about their work and seem willing and eager to see it tested on an international scale. The boldness and individuality of current Australian art mirrors the boundless vitality and variety of an Australian society in rapid flux, poised on the threshold of a new era.

Footnotes

1. Erasmus Darwin, "Visit of Hope" from *The Voyage of Governor Phillip to Botany Bay*, 1789, reprinted in Ian Turner, ed., *The Australian Dream*, New Zealand and Melbourne, 1968, p. 2.

2. Bill Hill, ed., *Australia Handbook 1983-1984*, Canberra, 1983, pp. 14-15.

BLEAK ROMANTICS

Memory Holloway

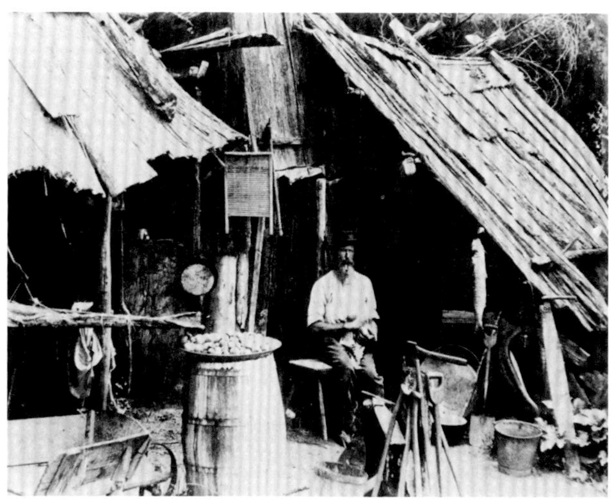

1 *Selector's Hut, East Gippsland, Victoria*
Collection La Trobe Library, State Library of Victoria,
Melbourne

Emblazoned across the center of a page of *The Sydney Morning Herald* recently was the pronouncement that "There simply is no clear national identity, and all attempts to fabricate one—whether by academics, cultural bureaucrats or advertisers — are false at least in part." Australia is only four years away from celebrating its bicentennial and this perhaps accounts to some extent for the nervous ticks that end in introspection and the search for self-definition. The point of departure — 1788 — is a dubious date to celebrate in any case. In January of that year the First Fleet sailed into what is now Sydney Harbor and emptied its human cargo — 565 male convicts, 192 women and eighteen children — onto Australian soil. From that moment on, those who arrived here and those generations to follow have attempted to assemble a puzzle of pieces that would define Australia.

Inventing Australia has been for over two hundred years a national obsession. Like the United States, Australia has been compelled to invent its own myths, to embark on a course that would lead to the final treasure—a clear picture of what Australia is, as a landscape, as a personality. For two hundred years the treasure chest has been plundered. Every decade or so a new set of bejeweled definitions was carted away as though a final truthful answer to the gnawing question had been found. "What is it to be Australian?"

In the 1980s we are still inventing that identity, though with less naiveté than before. There is by now a sense that our self-understanding is stuck together with collaged scraps from our own, European and American cultures. There is no one Australia. It is more accurate to view this place, its culture and its art, as Meaghan Morris has recently characterized it, as "a compilation culture of borrowed fragments, stray reproductions and alien(ated) memories … what we have *to begin with.*"[1] And to go from there.

Sticking bits together, improvising, making do has its own history in Australia: from the early evidence in settlers' homes made out of gigantic strips of eucalyptus bark, wedged together to form low-ceilinged shanties in the bush — to the great Australian Backyard — a conglomerate of tin-roofed outhouse, gardening shed, perhaps an unfinished boat, rusting barbeque, rotating Hill's Hoist clothesline (fig.1). It is a collage culture, built in response to a partial exposure to Western tradition. Aus-

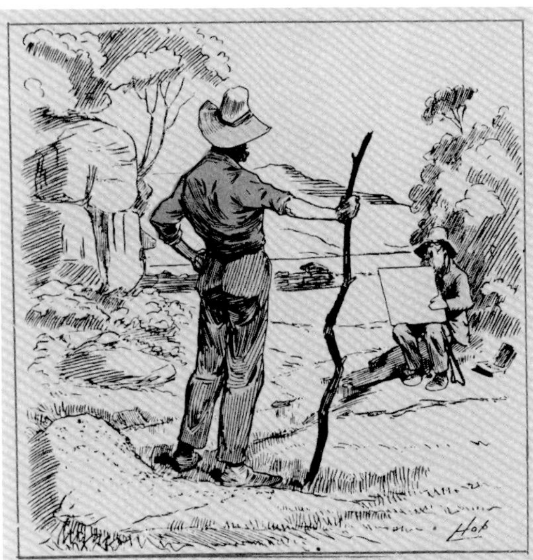

2 *Warming Enthusiasm*, ca. 1880-1900

tralian artists have responded accordingly, borrowing, cribbing from what they could see in State galleries and reproductions, stitching it all together into an uneven fabric that is stamped "Made in Australia."

Present-day art has been one among many modes whereby Australia has assembled and reassembled the pieces of a national identity, not into a unified whole (which can never exist anyway) but as a way of offering up another construction of reality. This art is both historically aware of its origins and wary of the cliché of Australian myths (primeval landscape, exotic flora and fauna, the "eternal" culture of aborigines) that have in the past left their stamp on images of Australia. The visual origins of Australian art lie in a mesh of popular imagery, for example the nineteenth-century black and white illustrations of magazines, such as *The Bulletin* (figs. 2,3). They lie also in the short tradition of Australia's art history — the romantic landscape fed by Germany and England, the Social Realism of the 1930s, the conscious cultivation of an Australian isolation in the late 1940s and 1950s, and since the 1960s the contagion of internationalism which at the end of the late decade left Australian art debilitated, with no direction in particular or too many in general.

Much has changed over the past six or so years to irrigate the channels of Australian art. The material conditions of Australian artists have altered. They now travel to Europe and America with greater frequency. They are included in large-scale shows to a greater extent than before (John Nixon at *Documenta 7* in 1983, Peter Booth at the Venice Biennale in 1982). Or they choose to live in several places at once (Dale Frank gives his current address as Vienna, New York and Singleton), or they take up resident scholarships in continental Europe rather than in England (Jan Murray is currently in Berlin on a Visual Arts Board grant). And then there is the tidal wave of artists, critics and curators who land in Sydney every two years for the Sydney Biennale, bringing with them art and ideas that are too often codified into a series of identifiable "house styles" by younger Australian artists who feel compelled to try on the new and the merging look from the Center.[2] Predictably enough the adaption is fragmented, partial, misunderstood — and consequently of interest because it holds up in relief the particular conditions of making art in Australia.

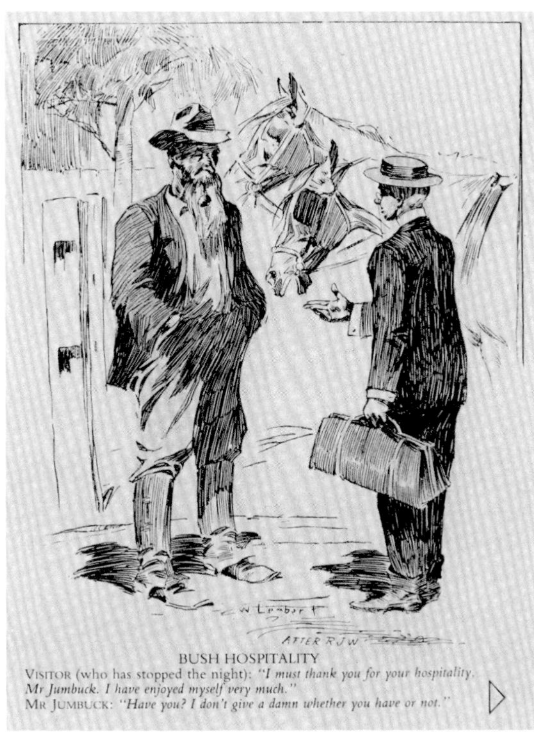

3 *Bush Hospitality,* ca. 1880-1900

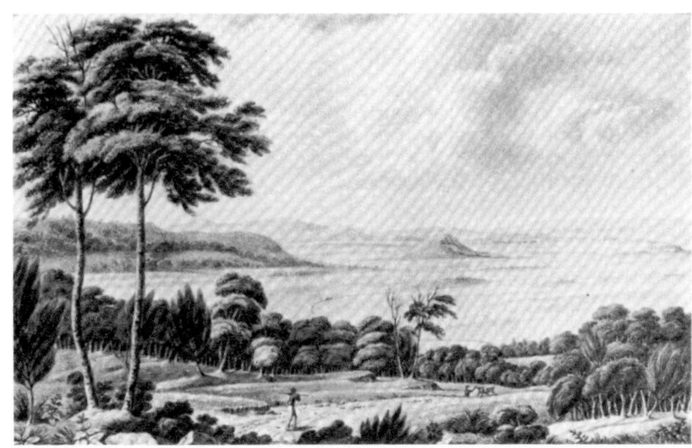

4 Joseph Lycett, *Salt Pan Plain, Van Diemen's Land*
Engraving from *Views in Australia,* 1824

Forced to acknowledge the authority of external cultures yet rooted in the experience of his own, the Australian artist takes up the mask of Janus: one face looks across the sea to search out contemporary models, the other looks back to a known terrain to reaffirm a sense of locality and self. In Australian art the landscape has been a staple diet for generations of artists. It provided a subject that defined and demarcated specific Australian experience. The bush, the harsh blinding light, the endless and monotonous spaces were the visual themes that eventually were so overused they came to represent a clichéd picture that no longer had vitality or validity. For many contemporary artists picturing the landscape is no longer an essential point of departure for self-definition, nor is it any longer the primary component in constructing a national identity.

To trace the response to the landscape is to begin to understand how Australia's self-image has changed over time. From the discovery of Australia each generation of artists has interpreted the landscape in terms of the predominant thought and events of the time. For the earliest explorers steeped in the Enlightenment, the landscape presented itself as a potential catalogue of scientific knowledge (fig. 4). Captain James Cook and botanist Joseph Banks postulated a landscape that could be controlled and humanized, Sydney Parkinson rendered the native plants and animals with strict scientific clarity and Joseph Lycett transformed the landscape into an Arcadian paradise. By the mid-nineteenth century this type of scientific enquiry gave way to the imagination, and the unfamiliar was made exotic, couched in a language of the sublime. Like many artists who arrived in Australia at the time, Eugene von Guérard, a pupil of the Düsseldorf School, did not come to paint but to find his fortune on the Ballarat gold fields in 1851. When that failed, he looked once again to the landscape, transforming it in his pictures into a vast silent space crammed with minutely observed details. Australia, *terra incognita,* was the ideal site where the imagination could work out its symbols of darkness and destructive power. When D. H. Lawrence arrived in Australia in 1922 it was this aspect of the bush that surfaced in *Kangaroo*:

*…the vast, uninhabited land frightened him. It
seemed so hoary and lost, so unapproachable….the
bush, the grey, charred bush. It scared him….It was*

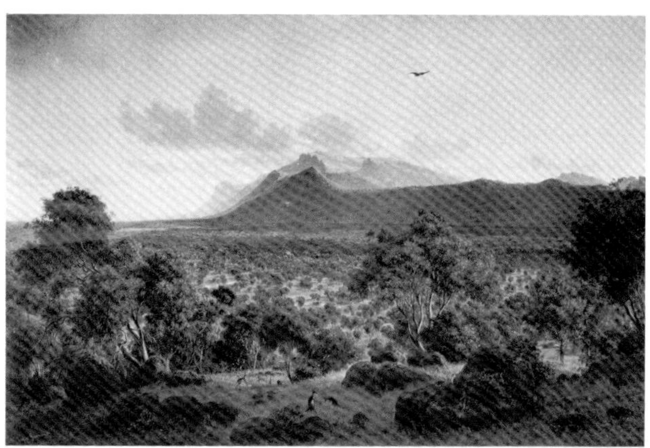

5 Eugene von Guérard, *Mt. William from Mt. Dryden,* 1857
Oil on canvas
Collection Art Gallery of Western Australia, Perth

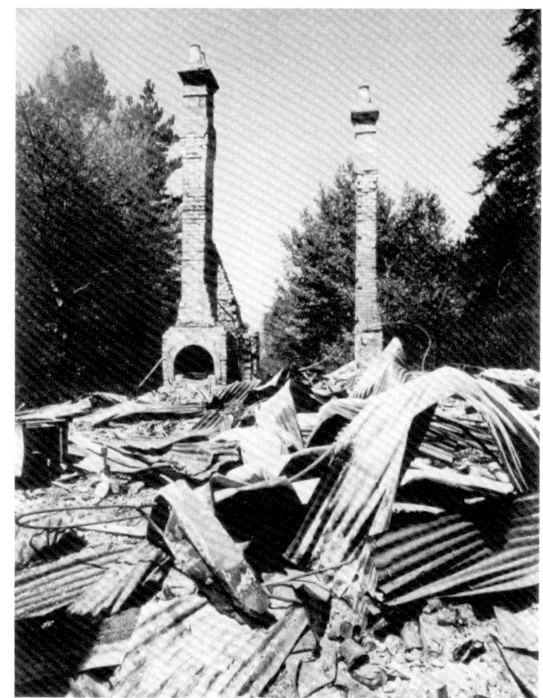

6 From *Ash Wednesday,* Adelaide and Melbourne, 1983,
n.p.

*so phantomlike, so ghostly, with its tall pale trees and
many dead trees, like corpses, partly charred by
bush fires.... And then it was so deathly still....He felt
it was watching, and waiting. Following with cer-
tainty, just behind his back. It might have reached a
long black arm and gripped him. But no, it wanted to
wait. It was not tired of watching its victim. An alien
people—a victim. It was biding its time with a terrible
ageless watchfulness....* [3]

Where does this leave the landscape and its use in the
1980s? For the eight artists here the landscape, over-
mythologized and too often the receptacle of stereotyped
visions, holds little direct attraction as a subject. The
painters of this generation speak of the landscape only
insofar as it is a backdrop against which they project their
understanding of Australia's cultural history, or they di-
vest it of its common attributes — heat and light — and
transform it into a darkened stage where menacing events
of the present are enacted.

To take three examples. Susan Norrie's *Lavished Living* (cat. no. 52) can be read in at least three ways: first,
as a tribute to von Guérard whose painting *Mt. William
from Mt. Dryden* of 1857 (fig. 5) appears as a panoramic
vista seen from the interior of a settler's hut. On another
level, Norrie's is an ironical observation on the monopoly
that landscape has had in Australian art. It has been at
the center of what has been seen and said about Australia
for two hundred years. Fanfare and dirge. With a single
blow Norrie delivers homage to the lingering power of the
myth of the landscape, and shows an intensely skeptical
mistrust of its grip on the imagination.

It is significant that Susan Norrie has chosen von Guérard, a German Romantic who saw in the Australian landscape the hand of God at work and the grandeur of nature
where man's labors left only marginal traces. The hut —
claustrophobic and domesticated with its lace curtain and
blue ribbon — is everything that nature is not. It is a col-
onized fragment of a threatening whole; an interior world
where refuge is taken against the outside. Her view of
civilization and the bush is very close to that of nineteenth-century artists and writers. By the early twentieth
century the convicts as well as the settlers were con-
sidered responsible for taming the landscape, thus legi-
timizing Australia's tainted history. In 1918 Mary Gilmore
wrote:

I was the conscript
  Sent to hell
To make in the desert
  The living well;

I split the rock;
  I felled the tree:
The nation was-
  Because of me.[4]

More recently Norrie has extended the opposition between the safe and the threatening to paintings that juxtapose the English garden with the wild landscape beyond. This is the image of an antipodean *hortus conclusus*: nature is all that is external to a wall that encloses the cultivated garden of civilization. Part of Norrie's cultural reckoning is formed from her need to understand her own family's place in Australia. Her father migrated from Cornwall in the 1930s and managed a large department store in Victoria. Norrie sees herself as the inheritor of English attitudes towards the Australian landscape as a spikey, dry wilderness. But as a first-generation Australian, she challenges that vision by replacing it with another, more contemporary view.

Lavished Living is also a critique of Australian materialism of a fantasized lifestyle based on women's magazines and a play on the title of *Vogue Living*. In those pages the luxury object triggers a string of associations that announce success, free time and possessions as ultimate goals. The guarantee of a lavish lifestyle is at odds with the former picture of Australia as a place of hardship but it is in keeping with a more recent notion of Australia as the Lucky Country.[5] The lace curtain in Norrie's painting represents an entire discourse on the Australian middle class—its attempts in the nineteenth century to reproduce the old country in a new and brutal one, its belief in objects as indicators of social position and, in the twentieth century, its gradual gentrification of the bush.

The luxury object has been until recently the principal subject of most of Norrie's paintings. Their titles, *Fruitful Corsage, Bridal Bouquet, Lingering Veils* (cat. no. 51), *Bequeathed Beaded,* refer to a suffocating world of the dressing table and wardrobe, an inner realm filled with sexual illusion. Diamonds and shells, overripe fruit and shimmering drapery are confined to airless spaces. The interior world is clogged, a stage where there is no room for movement. Unlike the paintings that look out onto a landscape, these are polished, reflective surfaces that mirror only their maker. Their romanticism resides in the contemplation of self and by extension in the symbols of personal fantasy and the dream. Narcissicism is an intensified search for cultural identity.

By its title Jan Murray's *The Three Graces* (cat. no. 32) alerts the viewer that it is a painting in part about classical civilization. The columns, the white drapery looped around the architectural supports as in an early Christian manuscript, and the fishes deposited at the bottom of the picture all indicate a network of pagan and Christian symbol. But there is more. There is also the landscape seared by the bush fires that hit Victoria and South Australia in the summer of 1983 (fig. 6). Several months later Murray visited these areas and painted *The Three Graces* partly in response to them. Like Susan Norrie's *Lavished Living*, Jan Murray's picture is a confluence of belief and doubt: belief in civilization and culture but also a doubt about the future existence of either. *The Three Graces* is a metaphor that displaces recent events too emotionally explosive to address directly. The landscape is intentionally fictionalized rather than reproduced.

The events that are suggested occurred as follows. On February 16, 1983, dotted areas throughout Victoria experienced the worst bush fires since 1939. Seventy-one people died, 1,719 homes were lost, 330,000 hectares destroyed and 25,000 stock wiped out. Richard Yallop of *The Age* described the early conditions that led to the fires. The day began with a temperature of 93.2 degrees, which rose by midday to 102.2 and by early afternoon to 105.8 and at 3:55 p.m. reached 109.4. A thirty-seven knot northerly carried the heat, and on the streets of Melbourne it was more like a blast furnace than an oven. An explosion of fires that hit towns in Victoria and South Australia followed. In some areas the fires raged for two days. Many died on the road while driving to escape. Anyone residing in either state at the time could not avoid the overpowering feeling of loss.

On a separate occasion after the fires Peter Booth also traveled to the burnt-out areas. Booth, whose work for the past six or so years has taken a grim view of the future, did a series of charcoal drawings of the scorched landscape around Warburton, one of the areas hit by the fires. Booth has used fire imagery consistently over a period of twenty years and it has a particularly poignant meaning for him, both as the focus for ritual and transformation and as a symbol of rejuvenation in nature. (It is common for Australian farmers to burn off parts of the bush to replenish the soil with nutrients. In northern New South Wales, an area Booth has visited on numerous occasions, and in Queensland, the canefields are prepared for harvesting by setting massive fires that drive out cane toads and snakes and destroy the undergrowth.) Among Booth's early memories are flames shooting out of the dark blast furnaces in Sheffield and the bombings during the war when the collective fear of fire and destruction was always present.

Transformation is a major key to Peter Booth's work and the changes endured by his figures could be likened to Ovid's observation in *The Metamorphoses* "Our own bodies too suffer a continual and interesting change, and the thing we were or are is not the thing we shall be tomorrow." Many of Booth's figures, the five-fingered homonculi, the hunchback, the animal-headed man, are in the process of transformation or they have already taken on the guise of monsters or devils. It is as though the mind has been exiled from the body and the irrational has taken over completely. Reason sleeps, monsters are produced. The specter of Goya is never far away. Booth makes these transformations work on several levels. The art of painting itself is a transformation of the material into the aesthetic. Booth's handling is expressive and calls attention to the surface irregularities much as he sets up for inspection the aberrations of human form. His color is carefully pared down to a few reds — sulphuric oranges set against grisaille or blackened backgrounds.

There is often a loosely structured narrative whose theme and figures are interchanged within groups of pictures: the "outsider" stands before the cheering crowd and becomes its leader; fires burn and figures dance around them like phantoms from a medieval dance of death; magicians and jugglers and deformed acrobats entertain by deceiving and dissembling. Man is metamorphosed into brute beast. Outsider, phantom, magician, beast are strung together to intone an overall message of the bizarre and dark aspects of human behavior. Life is presented as a carnival.

Darkness, skies shot with streaks of light, the industrial landscape devoid of human presence add up in Mandy Martin's paintings to a point of view that marks "the close of an era of civilization by destruction."[6] Martin is not alone in Australia in drawing parallels between mining, slag heaps, waste, wastefulness and a wasted civilization. (Jan Senbergs's *Mt. Lyell Copperopolis* paintings based on the mines in Tasmania draw similar attention to a decaying Western industrial state and the devastation left in its wake.) The threat works two ways: man wounds nature, and leaves scars; nature, with its droughts and fires strikes back. Martin is engaged with notions of survival. The rural landscape, so predominant in Australian art of the past, has been superseded by a dark horizon of smokestacks, lunar craters and mountains — the imaginary landscape of the future. Like her contemporaries in Europe and America she speaks of the drawing to a close of an era of civilization, and its possible destruction.

Mandy Martin has identified in these paintings a crucial shift in Australia's search for national identity and the country's changing economic realities. It was once said that Australia rides on the sheep's back. Today our future is dependent on mining instead of agriculture and Australia's economic health is tied to the outback — to the north and the west — rather than to industry in the cities. The outback — that perpetual red, dead center — is in the Australian imagination a crucial archetypal image. But the romanticism that once underpinned the fascination with the outback has now been replaced by hard economic fact. Australia is rephrasing her image for the world, an image that is rich in resources, to be sold off cheaply.

This bleak picture does not fit in with the myth of vast sunny skies, of razor-sharp shadows, of piercing sunlight and open space. Australia is not supposed to look like this. This is the country's answer to the northern Zeitgeist of the 1980s.

You're supposed to test the stereotypes, not devour them whole like a noon pie.

Barry Oakley, *Marsupials,* 1981

Know, O friendly generalizer that there be tall Australians and short Australians … faint or fierce, feeble, clinging or deathless strong … speculative, rash Australians; also cautious, very wary Australians…. There is no generic native Australian.

Rolf Bolderwood, "The Australian Native Born Type" in *In Bad Company and other stories,* 1901

It has been said often enough that Australian art today attempts to bring together personal identity and regional identity and that this search is in opposition to the blanket of international modernism that for fifteen years smothered a national Australian style. [7] Yet not one of the artists in the present exhibition feels compelled to define "Australianess" in their work.

Bill Henson's photographs of Australian crowds present the face of the country not as the sunburnt, male stereotype that was a common perception of the 1950s and the early 1960s, but as a multicultural urban society. Some figures: since 1947 immigrants and their offspring have accounted for over fifty percent of Australia's growth, and seventy percent of the growth of the work force. Over a quarter of the nation's population was born overseas and half of these immigrants are non Anglo-Saxon in origin. This means that now two out of every five Australians are either immigrants or children of immigrants, a proportion higher than that in the United States during its peak period of immigrant intake in the decade ending in 1910.

Immediately startling in Henson's photographs is how "un-Australian" they look, how European, specifically Mediterranean, his crowds are, and how much this shock of unfamiliarity reveals about our own self-perception. Henson is a Melbourne photographer. To identify this particular site of his practice is crucial. Nowhere else in Australia is the light so diffused, the sky so pearly when overcast. The city is dented by a large bay which funnels the winds from the south pole (or so it seems in mid-July). Melbourne is a winter city. (Sydney seems by comparison to be in a state of perpetual summer.) Henson's crowds are Melbourne crowds, photographed at a distance as

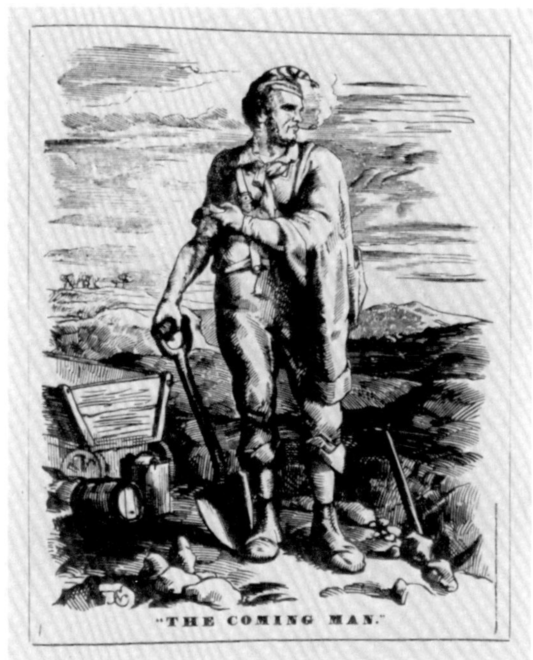

7 *The Coming Man,* from *Punch,* Melbourne, May 13, 1858, p. 133

they step from curbs and move along the main thoroughfare. They are presented outside history, outside any context other than the street, without personal attributes that might ascribe further meaning or supply additional information as to class or occupation. Henson describes rather than criticizes. He stands as the detached omnipotent camera eye that records in the Australian visage a state of anxiety and alienation characteristic of Western post-industrial society. In doing so he presents a new Australian type: urbanized, pessimistic, ensnared by the city and its tensions, a type whose pleasure is circumscribed by work and daily routine.

This is far from earlier construction of the Australian type and the Australian way of life. From the nineteenth century Australians have presented images of themselves as they wanted to be. [8] One of the earliest of these types was the "Coming Man" (fig. 7), an ennobled, independent and virile worker. At mid-century the national type was a white, male Anglo-Saxon who had preserved all the noble features of the British race. (Females were not characterized at all until the 1880s when they were likened to the independent "New Woman" in Britain.) Twenty years later, with the development of a self-conscious patriotism which began to manifest itself in gumnut architectural motifs and in literature, Australians began to view themselves as a healthier, more vigorous improvement on the initial stock. This superiority was in part attributed to the sunnier climate. In 1873 Anthony Trollope noted that the native-born colonist was superior to the English emigrant: "the best of our workmen go from us and produce a race superior to themselves."[9]

Then there were legendary figures — the bushman, characterized by Russell Ward in *The Australian Legend* as:

> *A practical man…a great improvisor…willing to "have a go" at anything but content with a task done in a way which is "near enough"…he feels no impulse to work hard…is taciturn, stoical and skeptical about the value of religion and of intellectual cultural pursuits generally.* [10]

Or the pioneer legend that fastened on the heroism, courageous feats and enterprising activities of the early pastoralist. These traits were made the subject of countless poems, especially in the 1890s by Banjo Paterson and Henry Lawson who emphasized mateship and egalitarianism. Both of these legends have been challenged since 1958 when Ward's book first appeared.[11]

There were other national types that took shape in the twentieth century: the Anzac, celebrated for his dogged perserverance at Gallipoli, the familiar cult of the Bondi beach lifesaver which emerged in the later 1930s ("there are no men in the world like your lifesavers," remarked an American observer at the time) and most recently the laid back, "she'll-be-right-mate" Ocker image, best expressed by Paul Hogan in his television advertisements selling cigarettes to Australians and Australia to Americans.

There still lingers the question of a national identity in the 1980s, which explains the sudden burst in the last four years of books and essays devoted to the topic. But if the search was marked in the 1960s by its high key of praise and optimism, it is now more sobering. Writing on national identity in *Intruders in the Bush*, sociologist John

Carroll has identified skepticism as the one character trait that is unique in its full form to Australia: "Australian skepticism has two strains, one dark and deeply pessimistic, without the dignity and idealism of tragedy; the other is more epicurean, carrying a jocular, light-hearted irreverence towards life."

These are the characteristics Bill Henson has frozen, but he has done so more as "bleak romantic" than skeptic. Transience, movement, flux and their imaginative transformation into form are part of a romantic legacy from which Henson draws. Most of his photographs are taken at rush hour. There is little sense of leisure as these figures move en masse towards their destinations somewhere in the work force or into the marketplace as consumers. Henson dramatically manipulates his darks and lights. He teases his figures out of the crowd, caresses the skin, makes it translucent like a finely grained marble. He stacks heads in isocephalic fashion as in an early Christian sarcophagus, thus concentrating on the state of mind rather than the body and by extension the body politic.

And what are we to make of the incursions of European nineteenth-century architectural façades, phrased like human heads and placed in juxtaposition to the Australian visage? It is here where face and façade meet that Henson fixes meaning. With a series of metonymies he makes explicit a chain of cultural links. Europe and its crumbling architecture — the bombed opera house of East Berlin, Viennese apartments, the area around the Berlin Wall— become the site of culture and civilization and its decay. Europe is static. Australia moves. Henson's longing for the past, his deliberate selection of an historicist architecture is the *Sehnsucht* of a romantic. He seeks to renew the old world by imaging the new one as an alternative that is in a state of perpetual movement.

Henson has said that his photographs are a microcosm of a macrocosm. They can be read individually as fragmented parts of a whole, or alternatively as an overall unity that builds towards its dramatic denouement in the final triptych. If we take them individually we underline their fragmentary quality — the head without torso, the hand which alone is expressive of a psychological state, the carrier bag inscribed with the names of cities of the world as a constant reminder of Australia's distance and isolation from those places. Taken collectively a murky narrative addressed to the topic of cultural identity and inheritance begins to form. Either way the work presents no false sense of optimism, nor does it engage with the heroic myths of the "young sunburnt country." It does present a romantic outlook that takes its pleasure in poetic speculation, in intuition and the triumph of individual imagination.

Individualism and stress on the subject as producer of meaning is treated by John Nixon in a way that separates him from the other artists in this exhibition. Since 1981 he has concentrated solely on making self-portraits based, as he says, on the avant-garde practice of Malevich, the Constructivists and Futurists as models. The cross that Nixon has assumed as an emblem stands in for the representational portrait and becomes the self-image. Nixon's strategy is the now familiar one of appropriating images from elsewhere, calling into question their original meaning and superimposing new interpretations. Nixon's practice is not strictly speaking one of pastiche or outright quotation so much as it is an aesthetic transformation and personalizing of already-known signs. The gesture, the variation of media as physical indicators of the artist's presence in the making of the work are crucial.

John Nixon's self-portraits are romantic and narcissistic in the way they obsessively center on the self. But they also present a decentered authorial voice. They are neither wholly mimetic nor entirely expressive (neither a mirror of reality nor a lamp illuminating it). They are fragments of a whole where each self-portrait can be seen as an individual work. But installed together they form one picture, one unity. They romantically reproduce the self yet they parody romantic introspection by relying on the imagery of the past and of others for their meaning.

John Nixon's work raises two important questions about the nature of art practice in Australia. First is the problem of originality which has particular bearing in a country where most international art, both past and present, is still seen in reproductions. Nixon is among those Australian artists who have made the best of these circumstances by opting for duplication, artistic parallels, parody and repetition as devices that bring into question the idea of originality. Nixon's references to historical precedents are significant in that he sees himself as continuing a minimal approach that reaches back through the 1960s in Australia and to the 1920s in Europe.

The possibility of an Australian *Tendenzwende*, where earlier native pictorial traditions might be mined for local subject matter, has been rejected by Nixon and others of his generation, although a group of younger artists in their early twenties is now using the expressionist work of Australians of the 1940s (one thinks especially of Albert Tucker, John Perceval, Arthur Boyd) as inspiration. At the moment Australian artists seem to take their cues from Europe and America or from aboriginal artifacts—a startling polarity. None of the artists represented here have used aboriginal art as a point of departure for their work. That was done by earlier generations of artists (Tony Tuckson, Ian Fairweather and more recently David Aspden and the sculptor John Davis) who found their way to abstract art by referring to aboriginal rituals and bark paintings as an Australian ur-abstraction.

The other question is that of the relationship between the fragment and the whole. Nixon's work is infinitely interchangeable. Inherent in this practice is a distrust of the finite object which extends to a suspicion of classical finish. The work of art conceived as a unity implies closure; fragments that can be arranged and rearranged can be read as notes on a lost original that recalls a more perfect utopian past.

Loosely defined, the self-portrait is also the subject of Dale Frank's drawings and paintings, but in its raw subjectivity it is at the opposite extreme from John Nixon's controlled, self-contained fragments. In a statement made in December 1982 Frank spoke of his work in terms of the "split image" and his art as "a protective puzzle (surrounding corridors, self images of desire)" and also of working with the Journey "which begins in darkness and melancholy." He has declared a sense of "urgency to find the Beast." Frank's words run parallel to the works themselves, and their echoes of psychoanalytic terminology and Surrealist fascination with the myth of the labyrinth and the minotaur (corridors, the Journey, the Beast) signal to the viewer an interpretive path that may be followed.

For the Surrealists who gave the title *Minotaure* to one of their diverse publications, the labyrinth was linked to the subconscious. The minotaur — half man, half beast — inhabited the inner reaches of the labyrinth and represented the tension between civilization and brutality, reason and the irrational. Frank's paintings are not overt illustrations of this theme but they are similarly immersed in the search for self-knowledge which entails traveling into unknown territory. Most important is the potential art offers as a way of making material the emotional intensity that search produces, or, as Frank has stated, the degree to which art is able "to harvest desire." And, one might add, to harness it in visual form.

To that end Frank stretches a taut network of lines out of which emerge apparitions that suggest the human head. Sometimes there is a double portrait with the implication of a split, schizoid self. In one such instance an open mouth appears to swallow (or disgorge?) another head. Concentric circles double as features of the face and body. Eyes and mouth are readily transformed into anus and vagina. These finely traced lines which expand and contract like magnetic fields bare the evidence of a struggle to give shape to idea. The obsessive fascination with filling the entire field is a convention that links these pieces to some symbolist art (one thinks of the sky in van Gogh's landscapes, the sinuous curves in Jan Toorop's work). But unlike van Gogh or Toorop, Frank rejects the possibility of mimesis as a means to indicate his interior states. Something deeper than surface reality is represented: inner tensions and an anxious searching. Merleau-Ponty has argued that every image exists for only the brief moment that precedes its own dispersal and collapse into another image, an interminable cycle of hallucination with no concession to reality. Frank's self-portraits need to be seen as images that flood into one another, images not framed or set apart, but images of flux and variations on one theme, the self.

For Australian artists the Journey is not only a metaphysical one where self-knowledge is the goal. The Journey towards and through northern continents is crucial in knowing what one has journeyed away from and what one is returning to. "Being Australian," as one of Barry Oakley's characters observes in the play *Marsupials*, "is a kind of painless disease — it doesn't start to hurt until you leave the place." At one time just after the second war Australian artists left without returning or they exiled themselves for as long as a decade.

The Journey then had a fixed goal, to seek a more hospitable cultural climate; the uphill climb away from an indifferent Australia seemed more arduous, but also more definitive. Those artists of the 1940s and 1950s could emerge from their steep ascent to look back over a terrain where others were in various stages of escape. The only cure for "the painless disease" then seemed to be to stay away. Forty years later the periods of exile are briefer, the stay (six months is the average now) is punctuated with exhibitions and occasional acknowledgement with invitations to become artists in residence or to take up foreign grants. The Journey is no longer an ascent; it is circular and involves going and coming many times, with all the uncertainty and divided loyalties such travel implies.

For many young Australian artists the Journey is a significant theme that expresses the ambivalence about being in Australia. Dale Frank uses the voyage as a way of entering the body and the mind. (When Freud made the analogy between the labyrinth and the intestines he drew attention to the Journey as a metaphor for interior search.) But the Journey for Frank is also a real one. He lives most of the time outside Australia and like Bill Henson has exhibited less in Australia than overseas. "Three months in Australia is enough."

Jan Murray uses the Journey metaphorically to comment on the passage "from the past into the future. My paintings are about journeys and discoveries ... about hope against doom...." She assembles in them fragments of European culture and Christian iconography. Classical temples are menaced with destruction, fishes are crucified, the land is threatened by holocaust, heads are severed and the world appears to be on the verge of disappearing down a vortex. Murray surrounds herself with emblems of entrapment and escape. Nets and tanks catch and contain, figures are bound with rope. Boats and water and ladders provide the means to flee. These are oblique references to what it feels like to paint and to be in Australia.

And how is one to use Western tradition, how to address the past, the legacy of Europe and the myths of Australia? Jan Murray refers to a European figurative tradition of the past, especially to Max Beckmann. In one of her paintings a bound figure sits like a mute and headless Ned Kelly (the antihero who is symbol in Australia of rebellion and independence), thrust out to sea with his companions. European tradition casts a long shadow in Australia. It can be a devastating force that prevents the individual from coming to terms with the present and one might add, with a sense of place. Although there is little that is identifiably Australian in this work, no sunny landscapes, furry koalas, no tall sad gum trees or deserted towns of the outback, the underlying themes of the voyage, the traps, the escape across water to another land, are indeed themes of our own time and place.

Escape takes another form in the small panel paintings of Vivienne Shark LeWitt. The scale of the works is intimate (like much postmodernist art), their content is structured by making myth out of personal experience, and their style is organized around an ironic use of Pre-Raphaelite figures, Gothick narrative on good and evil and medieval allegory. Several of these paintings are diptychs and their physical division into two parts is reinforced by the play of opposites: good and evil, or beauty and ugliness. In *Charles Meryon the Voyeur. La Belle et la bête* (cat. no. 55) male bestiality sits in opposition to female fear. He holds a gun, she a sword; he is painted against a drab neutral ground, she stands in a flood of red. Violation is by the gaze that is sanctioned by society. The atmosphere of threat, the sense of being watched from behind supply the tone of voyeurism that appears in this and other pictures by Shark LeWitt.

Although these are not explicitly feminist narratives, they do address the experience of women. *The Bloody Chamber* (cat. no. 54), taken from a short story by Angela Carter, presents a sequence in which Taurus pushes a woman from a window. She submits, is subdued and finally overcome by the beast.

Flight, a longing for another place, the fascination with ruins and fragments, this is the armature of a romantic outlook seen repeatedly in this exhibition. While romanticism is the underlying sensibility, it is wary, knowing, bleak. This latter-day romanticism seeks not to be at one with the universe or the land, nor does it set out to transcend contemporary life. There are moments of visionary consciousness. But the heroes and heroines of these paintings and photographs are not mythical cultural figures as they might have been forty years ago.

In our Journey we are at a crossroads. We have left behind old myths (of mateship and egalitarianism) only to invent new ones yet to be defined and tested. It appears that once again we are in search of an identity and as in the past this search is precipitated by Australia's desire to measure itself against Europe and America. This time that definition may be at odds with the popular conception of Australia as hedonistic haven or the last frontier. And instead we just might begin to see ourselves as through a prism: a culture shot through with difference and contradiction, an urban polyglot nation that hangs precariously but tenaciously to the edge of civilization.

Footnotes

1. Meaghan Morris, *D'un autre continent: l'Australie. Le rêve et le réel*, exh. cat., Paris, 1983, p. 39.

2. Nelly Richard has identified similar patterns of resistance and absorption in Latin American work in "Latin America: Cultures of Repetition or Cultures of Difference?," *The Fifth Biennale of Sydney. Private Symbol: Social Metaphor*, exh. cat., Sydney, 1984, n.p.

3. D.H. Lawrence, *Kangaroo*, London, 1923, reprinted 1970, pp. 8-9.

4. Mary Gilmore, *The Passionate Heart*, Sydney, 1918, n.p.

5. Donald Horne, *The Lucky Country: Australia in the Sixties*, Harmondsworth, 1966.

6. Statement by the artist in conversation with the author.

7. Léon Paroissien, *D'un autre continent: l'Australie. Le rêve et le réel,* pp. 26-31.

8. Richard White, *Inventing Australia: Images and Identity 1688-1980*, George Allen and Unwin, Sydney, 1981, pp. VIII-X.

9. Anthony Trollope, *Australia and New Zealand*, vol. I, London, 1873, p. 168.

10. Russell Ward, *The Australian Legend*, Oxford, 1958.

11. John Carroll, ed., *Intruders in the Bush: The Australian Quest for Identity*, Melbourne, 1982, and Michael Roe, "The Australian Legend," *Meanjin*, vol. 21, no. 3, 1962, pp. 363-369.

PETER BOOTH

Born in Sheffield, England, 1940

Sheffield College of Art, 1956-57

Works at various jobs in Melbourne, 1958-62

National Gallery School, Melbourne, 1962-65

Prize for Subject Painting; joint recipient of Bernard Hall Prize for Figure Painting, National Gallery School, 1964

Teaches painting at Prahran Technical College, Melbourne, 1966-69

Teaches drawing part-time at National Gallery School, 1967

Works at various jobs in Melbourne, 1967-69

Lives in Melbourne

Selected Group Exhibitions

National Gallery of Victoria, Melbourne, *The Field,* August-September 1968. Catalogue with texts by Brian Finemore and John Stringer. Traveled to Art Gallery of New South Wales, Sydney, October-November 1968

Art Gallery of New South Wales, Sydney, *Recent Australian Art,* October-November 1973

Archibald Fountain, Hyde Park, Sydney, *The Philip Morris Arts Grant 2nd Annual Exhibition 1975*, March-April 1975

National Gallery of Victoria, Melbourne, *Minimal Art*, February-March 1976

George Paton Gallery, University of Melbourne, *Drawing: Some Definitions*, June 1976

George Paton Gallery, University of Melbourne, *Minimal Art*, July 1976

Art Gallery of New South Wales, Sydney, *Biennale of Sydney: European Dialogue*, April-May 1979. Catalogue

University Gallery, University of Melbourne, *Melbourne/ Monash Exchange Exhibitions*, February 1980. Checklist with texts by Jenefer Duncan and R.D. Marginson. Traveled to Monash University Gallery, Melbourne, March-April

Visual Arts Board, Regional Development Program No. 7, Sydney, *In the Labyrinth* (with Mike Brown), opened September 1980. Catalogue with text by Gary Catalano. Traveled in Australia until May 1981

Art Gallery of New South Wales, Sydney, *Some Australian Drawings, 1880-1980*, May-June 1981

Art Gallery of New South Wales, Sydney, *Australian Perspecta 1981: A biennial survey of contemporary Australian art*, May-June 1981. Catalogue with text by Bernice Murphy

Royal South Australian Society of Arts Gallery, Adelaide, *Spectres of our Time*, August 1981

Serpentine Gallery and Institute of Contemporary Art, London, *iEureka! Artists from Australia*, March-April 1982. Catalogue with text by Nancy D.H. Underhill

Venice, *La XL Biennale di Venezia: Visual Arts 82*, June-July 1982. Catalogue with text by Gary Catalano; portion reprinted as "Les Images de terreur de Peter Booth," *Art Press*, October 1983, pp. 26-27. Australian section traveled to National Gallery of Victoria, Melbourne, as *Australia at the 1982 Venice Biennale: Works by Peter Booth and Rosalie Gascoigne*, November 1982-January 1983

National Gallery of Victoria, Melbourne, *The Seventies: Australian Paintings and Tapestries from the Collection of the National Australia Bank*, October-November 1982. Catalogue with text by Robert Lindsay

Art Gallery of New South Wales, Sydney, *Project 40: Australian Artists at Venice and Kassel*, February-March 1983. Catalogue with text by Bernice Murphy

ARC/Musée d'Art Moderne de la Ville de Paris, *D'un autre continent: l'Australie. Le rêve et le réel*, October 4-December 4, 1983. Catalogue with text by Suzanne Pagé and Léon Paroissien

Art Gallery of South Australia, Adelaide, *Recent Australian Painting: A Survey 1970-1983*, December 1983-February 1984. Catalogue with text by Ron Radford

National Gallery of Victoria, Melbourne, *Vox Pop*, December 1983-February 1984. Catalogue with text by Robert Lindsay

Art Gallery of New South Wales, Sydney, *The Fifth Biennale of Sydney. Private Symbol: Social Metaphor*, April-May 1984

Selected One-Man Exhibitions

Pinacotheca, Melbourne, March-April 1969; August-September 1970; September 1971; August 1972; August 1975; November 1976; November 1977; October 1978; November 1979; November 1980; November 1981; November-December 1982; November 1983 (drawings)

Central Street Gallery, Sydney, April-May 1969

Chapman Powell Gallery, Melbourne, May 1973; April 1974

Art Gallery of New South Wales, Sydney, *Project 12: Peter Booth*, March-April 1976. Checklist with text by Frances Lindsay

Monash University Gallery, Melbourne, *Peter Booth: A Retrospective*, May 1976

Selected Bibliography

Interview with Bruce Pollard, "Peter Booth: The Distance is Closer," *Source,* September 7, 1971, p. 30

Graeme Sturgeon, "Arts Review," *The Australian*, May 25, 1976, p. 20

Graeme Sturgeon, "Arts Review," *The Australian*, November 20, 1976, p. 20

Mary Eagle, *The Age*, October 4, 1978, p. 2

Frances Lindsay, "Peter Booth," *Art and Australia*, vol. 16, no. 1, 1978, pp. 47-54

Janine Burke, "Art for the End of the World," *Meanjin*, vol. 40, October 1981, pp. 375-388

Bernice Murphy, "Painting," *Australian Art Review*, October 1981, pp. 30-31

Nick Waterlow, "Australian Perspecta 1981: A biennial survey of contemporary Australian art," *Australian Art Review*, October 1981, pp. 84-85

Jennifer Phipps, "Flash Art Australia: Peter Booth," *Flash Art*, December 1981-January 1982, p. 60

Paul Taylor, "Angst in My Pants," *Art & Text,* September 1982, pp. 48-60

Robert Rooney, "Arts Review," *The Weekend Australian*, November 27-28, 1982, p. 27

Memory Holloway, *The Age*, December 1, 1982, p. 14

Helen Topliss, "Leaves from a Dream Diary. A Note on the Art of Peter Booth," *Helix*, no. 11-12, 1982

Nancy D.H. Underhill, "40 ans d'art en australie," *Art Press*, October 1983, pp. 21-22

Jill Montgomery, "AUSTRALIA—The French Discovery of 1983," *Art & Text,* January 1984, p. 13

Jennifer Phipps, "Entre deux Mondes—Australians in Paris," *The Age Monthly Review,* vol. 3, January 1984, p. 13

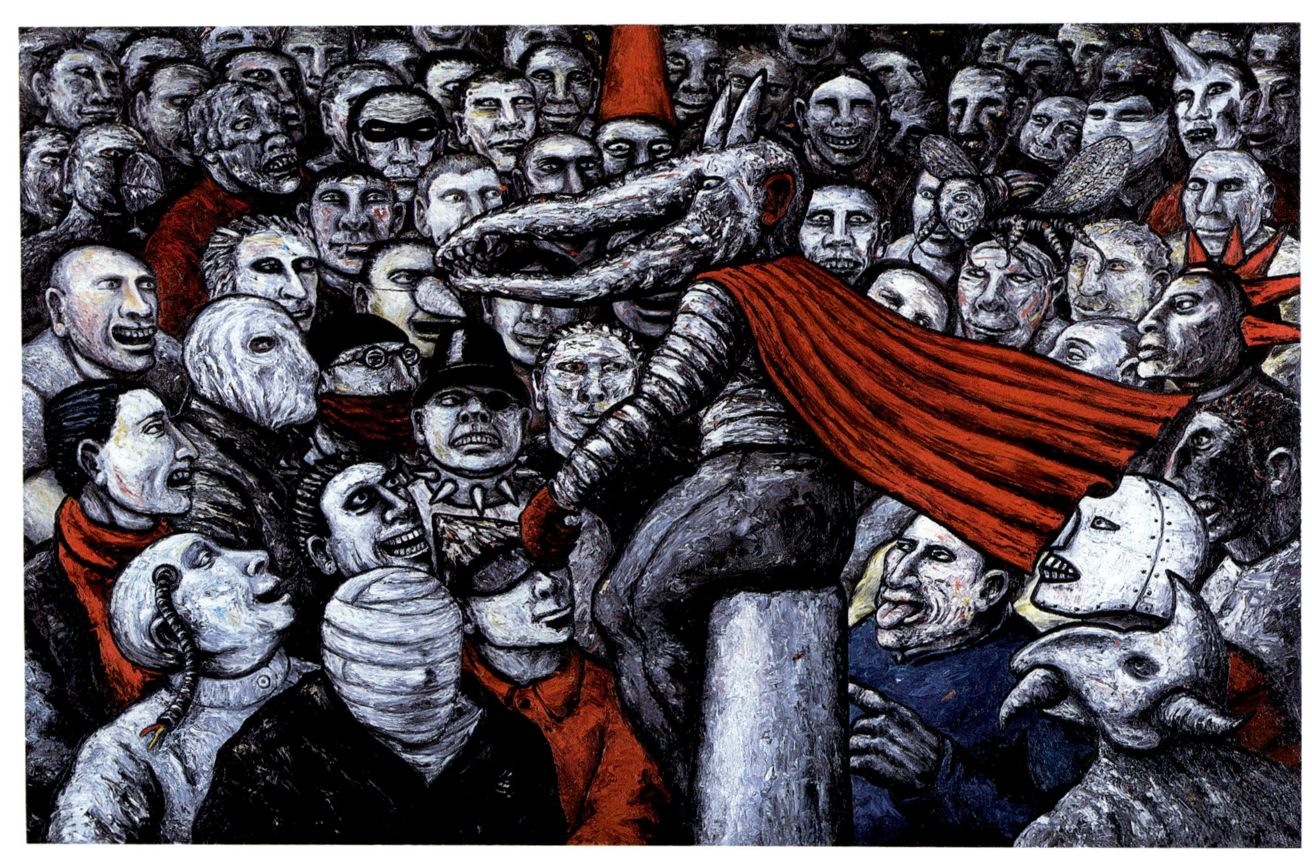

1 | *Painting 1981.* 1981
Oil on canvas, 77¾ x 119⅞″ (197.5 x 304.5 cm.)
Collection Art Gallery of New South Wales,
Sydney; purchased with the assistance of the
Visual Arts Board, Australia Council, 1981

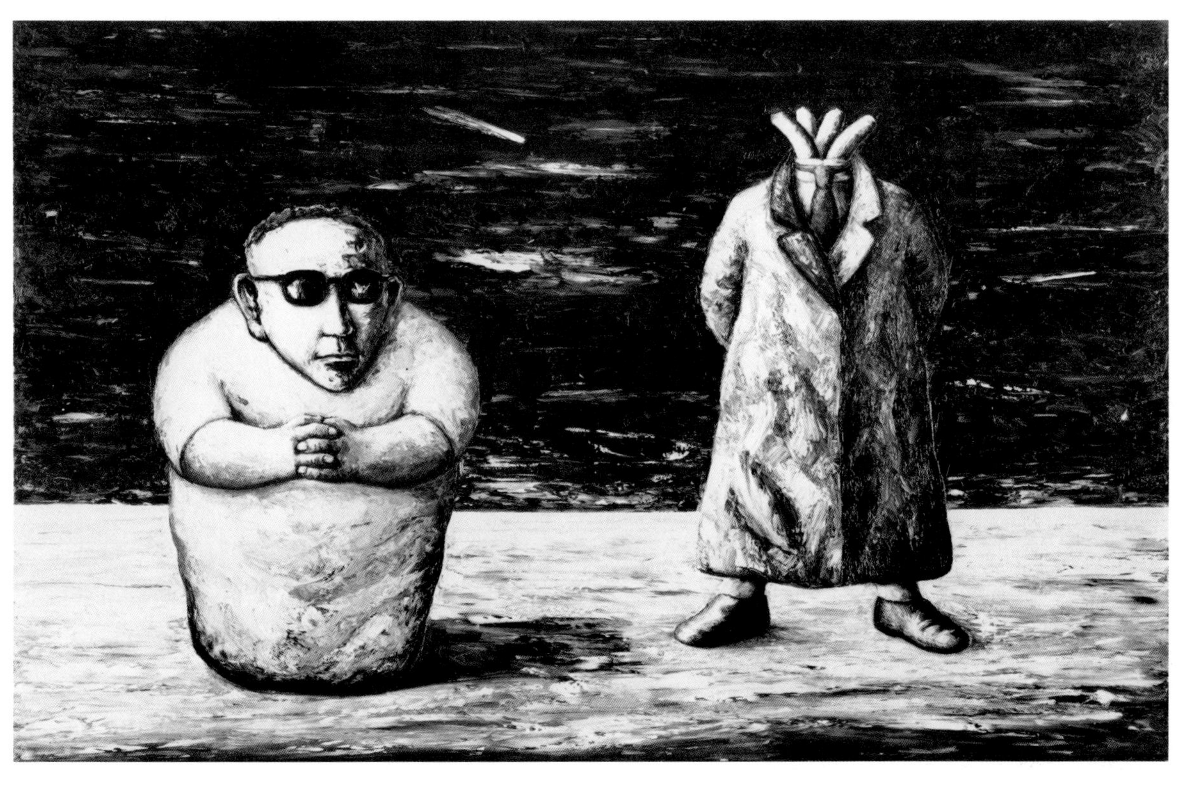

2 | *Painting 1982.* 1982
Oil on canvas, 66⅞ x 102⅜″ (170 x 260 cm.)
Collection Michael Darling

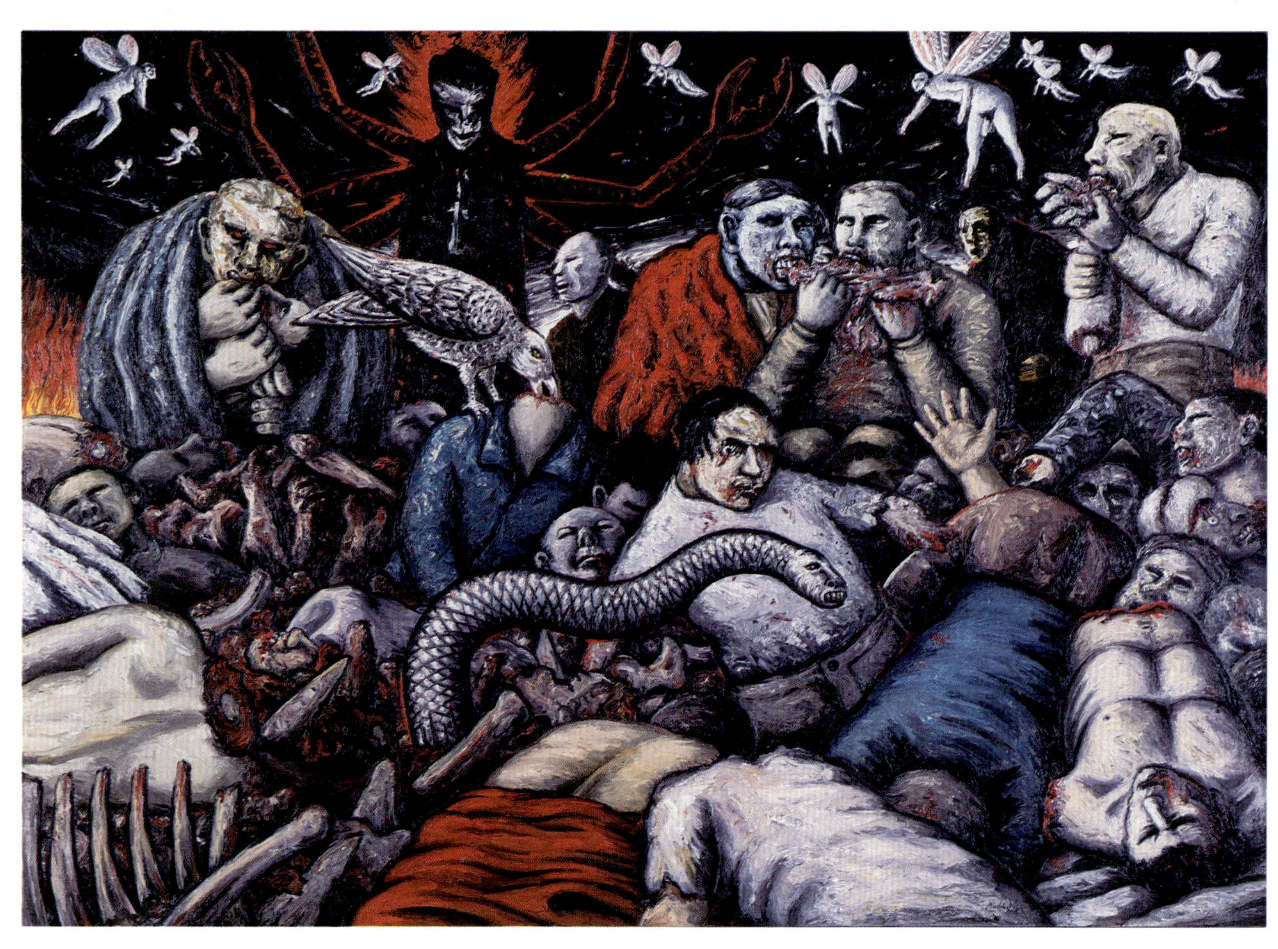

3 | *Painting 1982.* 1982
Oil on canvas, 77⅞ x 107⅞" (197.7 x 274 cm.)
Collection Art Gallery of South Australia,
Adelaide; A.M. Raglass Bequest Fund, 1983

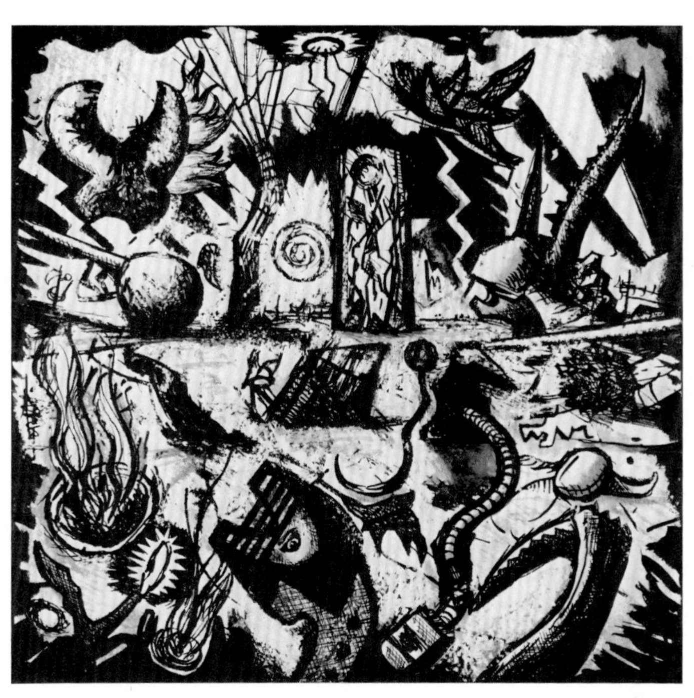

4 | *Drawing 1983.* 1983
Ink, chalk and ink wash on paper, 7¾ x 7¾"
(19.8 x 19.8 cm.)
Courtesy Pinacotheca, Melbourne

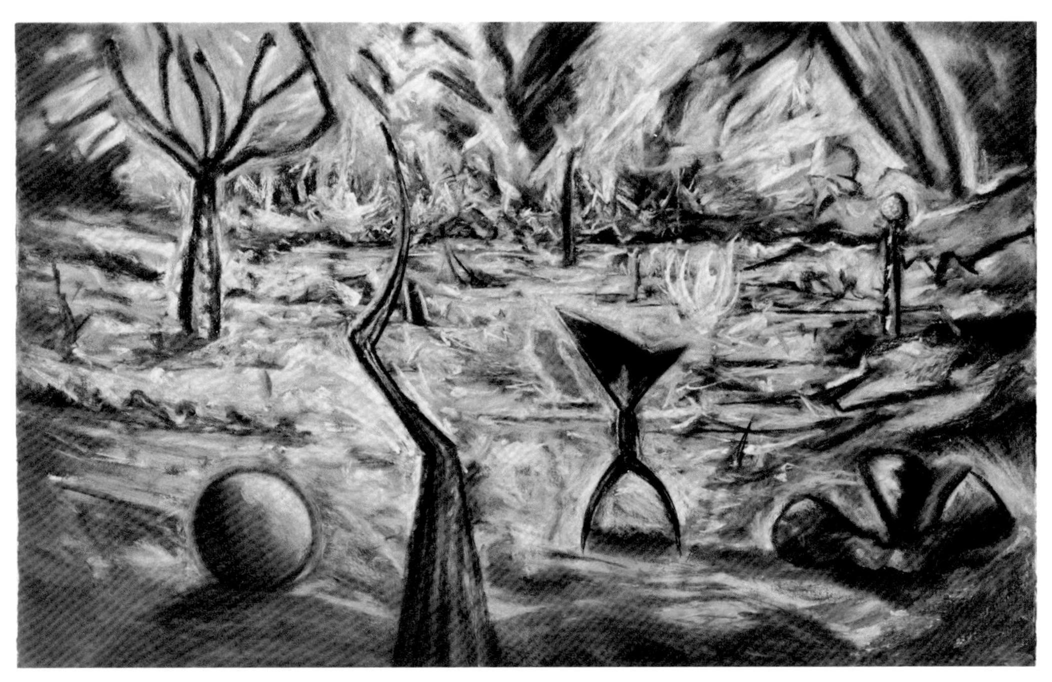

5 | *Drawing 1984.* 1984
Pastel on paper, 26 x 41″ (66 x 104 cm.)
Courtesy Pinacotheca, Melbourne

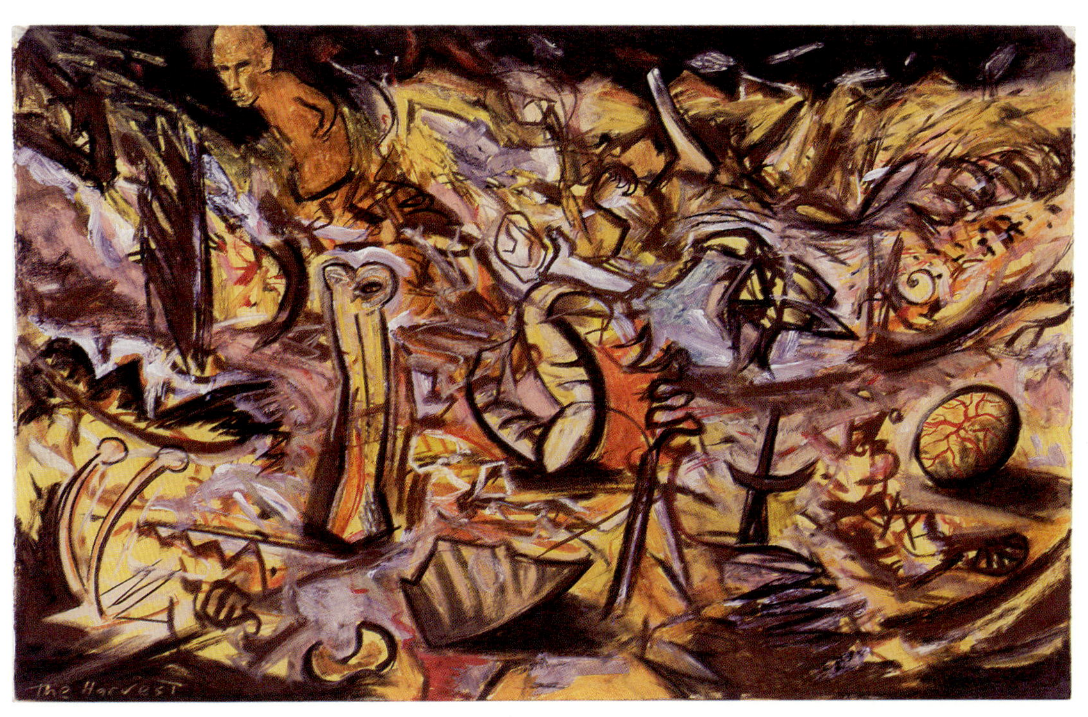

6 | *Drawing 1984 (The Harvest).* 1984
Pastel and gouache on paper, 26 x 41″
(66 x 104 cm.)
Courtesy Pinacotheca, Melbourne

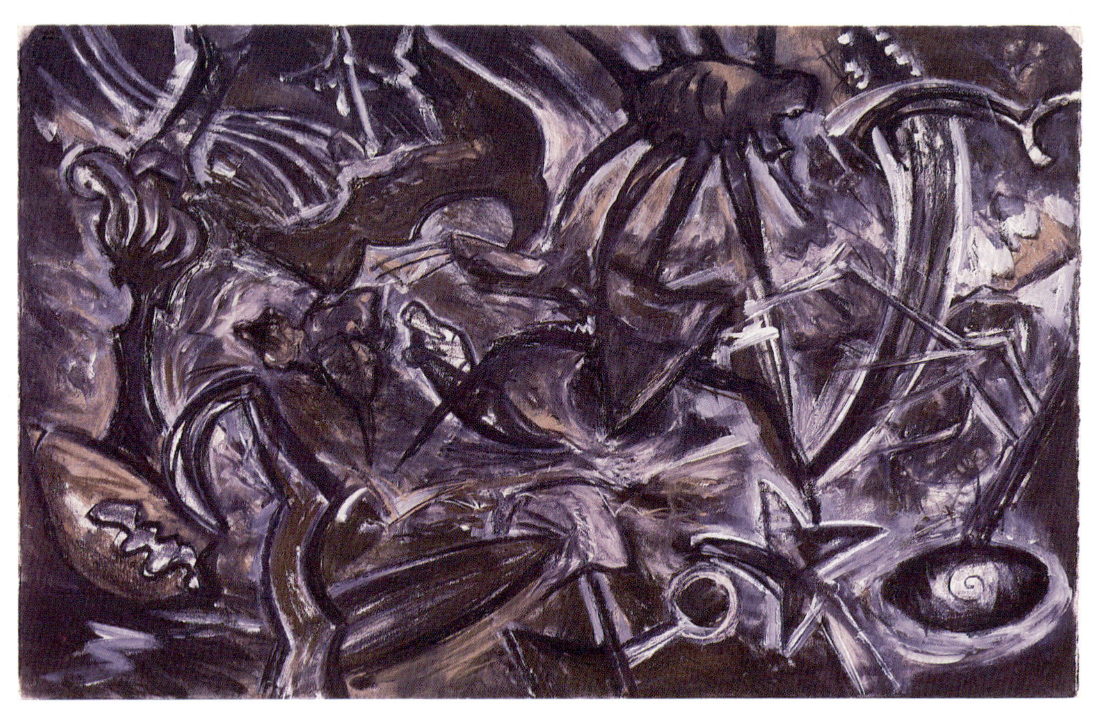

7 | *Drawing 1984.* 1984
Pastel and gouache on paper, 26 x 41″
(66 x 104 cm.)
Courtesy Pinacotheca, Melbourne

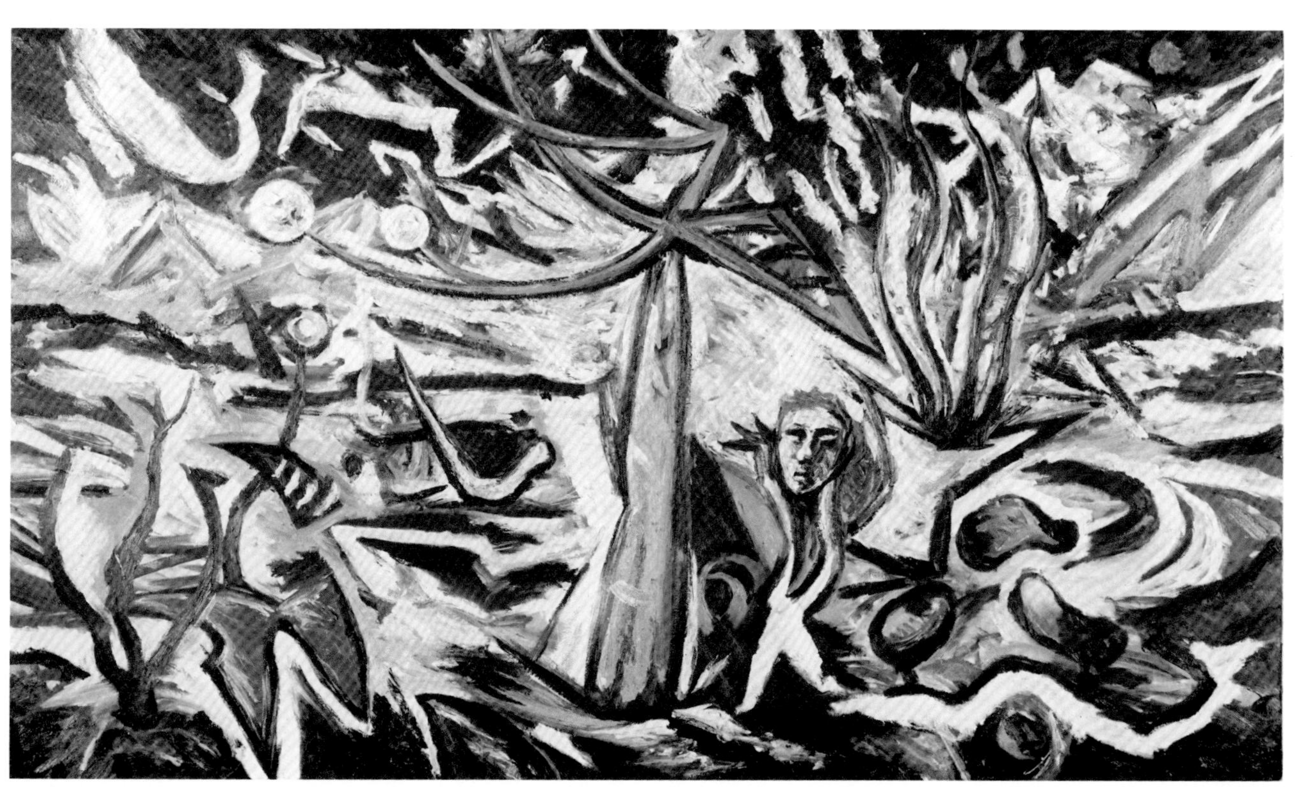

8 | *Painting 1984.* 1984
Oil on canvas, 72 x 120″ (182.8 x 304.8 cm.)
Courtesy Pinacotheca, Melbourne

DALE FRANK

Born in Singleton, New South Wales, 1959

Self-taught as an artist

Lives in Singleton, Adelaide and Sydney until 1979

Lives primarily in Europe (Ireland, The Netherlands, Belgium and Italy) and New York, with several months each year in Australia, 1979-present

Currently lives in Vienna, New York and Singleton

Selected Group Exhibitions

P.S. 1, Institute for Art and Urban Resources, New York, *April Show*, April-May 1981

Espace Lyonnais d'Art Contemporain, Lyon, *Les Oeuvres plastiques*, May 1981

Galleria Pellegrino, Bologna, *Group Show*, May 1981

Robert McDougall Art Gallery, Christchurch, New Zealand, *ANZART, Australia/New Zealand Encounter*, August 1981

Art Gallery of New South Wales, Sydney, *Biennale of Sydney: Vision in Disbelief,* April-May 1982. Catalogue with texts by Elwyn Lynn and William Wright

Willard Gallery, New York, *White and Black Drawings* (with Susan Rothenberg), December 1982

Museo Palazzo Lanfranchi, Pisa, *Panorama della Post-Critica* (with Thomas Lawson and Anselm Kiefer), February-March 1983. Catalogue with text by Helena Kontova

University Gallery, University of Melbourne, *Tall Poppies: An exhibition of five pictures,* April-June 1983. Catalogue with text by Paul Taylor; reprinted as "Tall Poppies," *Art & Text*, January 1984, p. 52

Art Gallery of New South Wales, Sydney, *Australian Perspecta 1983: A biennial survey of contemporary Australian art*, May 12-June 26, 1983. Catalogue with text by Bernice Murphy and Janet Parfenovics

Gimpel Fils Gallery, London, *Place*, June-July 1983

Galerie t'Venster, Rotterdam, and Bonnefantenmuseum, Maastricht, The Netherlands, *De Goddelijke Komedie*, September-November 1983. Catalogue with text by Paul Groot

ARC/Musée d'Art Moderne de la Ville de Paris, *D'un autre continent: l'Australie. Le rêve et le réel*, October 4-December 4, 1983. Catalogue with texts by Suzanne Pagé and Léon Paroissien

Art Gallery of South Australia, Adelaide, *Recent Australian Painting: A Survey 1970-1983*, December 1983-February 1984. Catalogue with text by Ron Radford

National Gallery of Victoria, Melbourne, *Vox Pop*, December 1983-February 1984. Catalogue with text by Robert Lindsay

Venice, *La XLI Biennale di Venezia: Aperto-84, Arte e Arti, Attualità e Storia*, June-August 1984

Selected One-Man Exhibitions

Performances, Adelaide, Singleton, Dublin, Belfast, Amsterdam, Warsaw, Budapest, Milan, London, 1977-79

Experimental Art Foundation, Adelaide, September 1979

Galerie Dany Keller, Munich, October 1980

Kunstlerhaus, Hamburg, November 1980

Acme Gallery, London, January 1981

P.S. 1, Institute for Art and Urban Resources, New York, September-October 1981

Galleria Pellegrino, Bologna, November 1981

Galerie Tanit, Munich, February 1982

Die Internationale Kunstmesse, Basel, *Perspektive 13 '82*, June 1982

Roslyn Oxley9, Sydney, August-September 1982; August-September 1983; June-July 1984

Galerie Severina Teucher, Zürich, December 1982-February 1983

Museum Fodor, Amsterdam, March-April 1983

Studio d'Arte Cannaviello, Milan, May-June 1984

University Gallery, University of Melbourne, July 31-August 31, 1984. Catalogue with text by Paul Groot

Selected Bibliography

Helena Kontova, "From Performance to Painting," *Flash Art*, February-March 1982, pp. 16-21

Roberto Daolio, "Dale Frank, Artista," *Lapis Arte*, June 1982, pp. 8-10

Marcia Tucker, "An Iconography of Recent Figurative Painting: Sex, Death, Violence and the Apocalypse," *Artforum*, vol. XX, June 1982, pp. 31-33

Mike Parr, "Glossolalia/Stroke: (The Art of Dale Frank)," *Aspect*, no. 25, Spring 1982, pp. 60-63

Mike Parr, "Vision in Disbelief: 4th Biennale of Sydney," *Flash Art*, June-July 1982, pp. 71-72

Jennifer Phipps, "ANZART," *Australian Art Review*, 1982, p. 81

[Review], *Domus*, no. 629, 1982, p. 74

Bernice Murphy, "Recent Painting in Australia," *Flash Art*, January 1983, pp. 56-59

Matthew Collings, "Place at Gimpel Fils," *Artscribe*, September 1983, pp. 61-62

Paul Groot, "Museum Fodor Exhibition," *Flash Art*, September 1983

Ashley Crawford, "Dale Frank," *Tension*, October 1983

Vivienne Shark LeWitt, "The End of Civilization, Part II: Love Among the Ruins," *Art & Text,* no. 10, 1983, pp. 1-7

Interview with Helena Kontova, *Flash Art,* September 1984

Jenny Watson, "Urgent Images," *Art & Text,* Winter 1984, p. 69

Stuart Morgan, "Dale Frank," *Artforum*, forthcoming in 1984.

9 *The miner's rich vein and a double portrait of a possible miner from the front. Triple portrait.*
1983
Acrylic on canvas, 68⅞ x 100″ (175 x 254 cm.)
Collection National Gallery of Victoria, Melbourne; purchased with funds from Michell Endowment, 1983

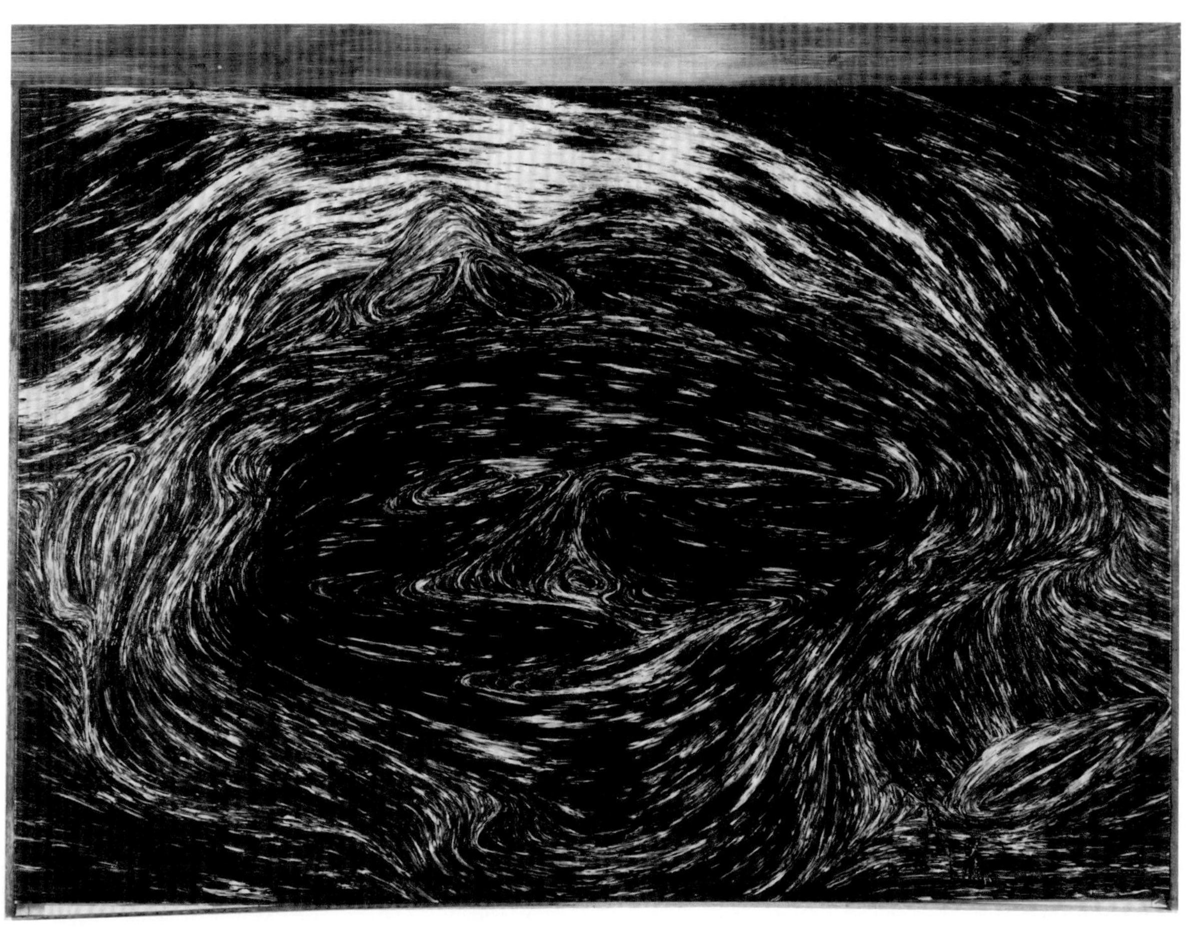

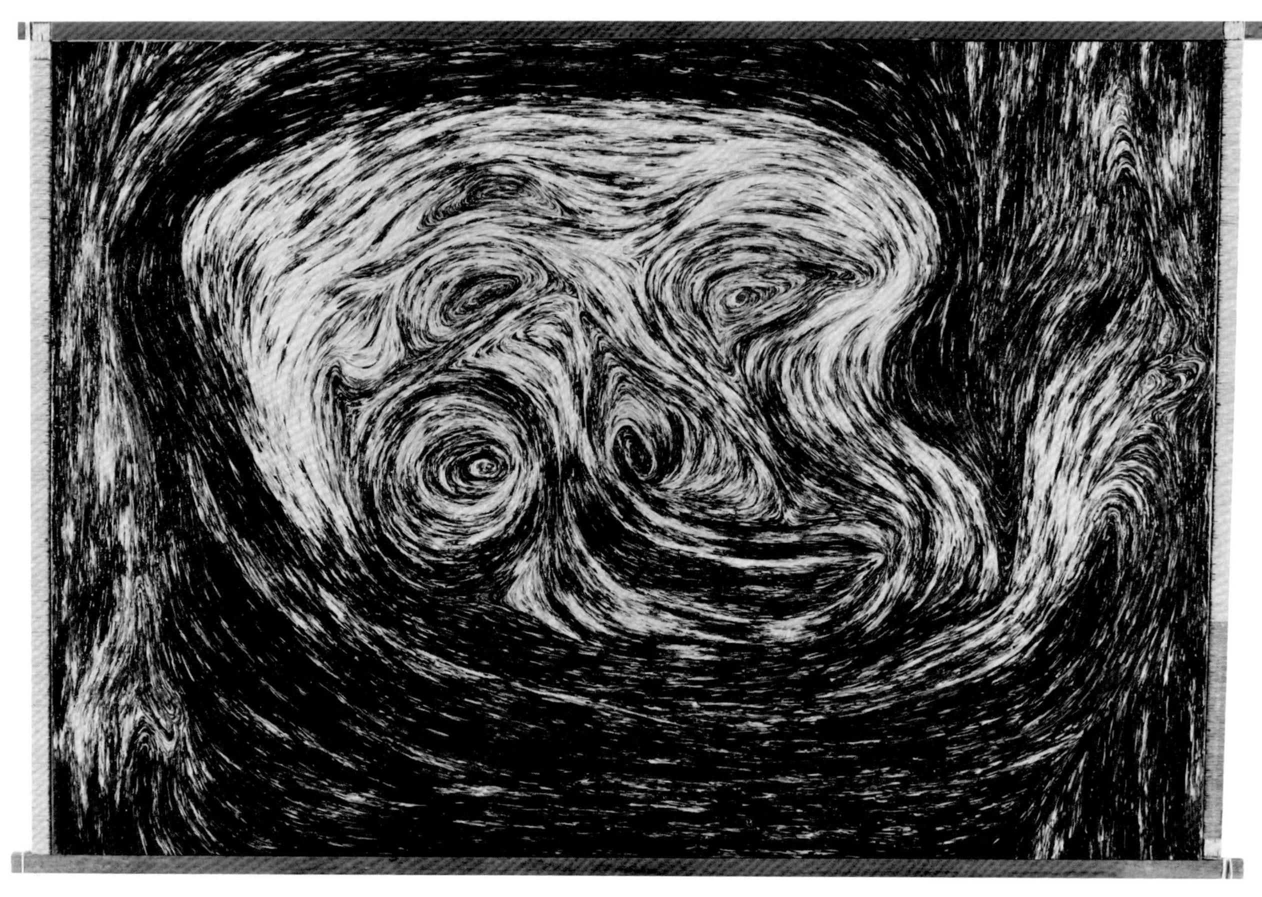

10 *Self portrait. The snail fleeing. An attempt to be sensible. And a portrait of Paul Groot.* 1983
Acrylic on canvas, 68⅞ x 98⅞″ (175 x 251 cm.)
Collection Art Gallery of South Australia, Adelaide

36

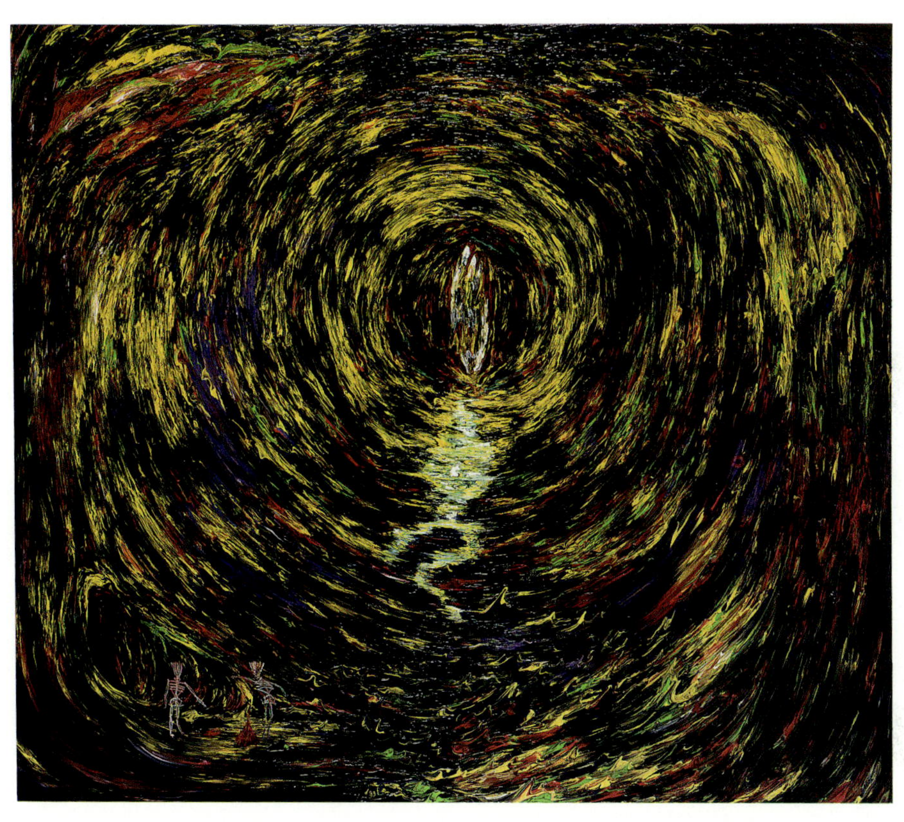

11   *The evil seepage and the miner's escape.* 1983
Acrylic on canvas, 70⅞ x 78¾" (180 x 200 cm.)
Courtesy Roslyn Oxley9, Sydney

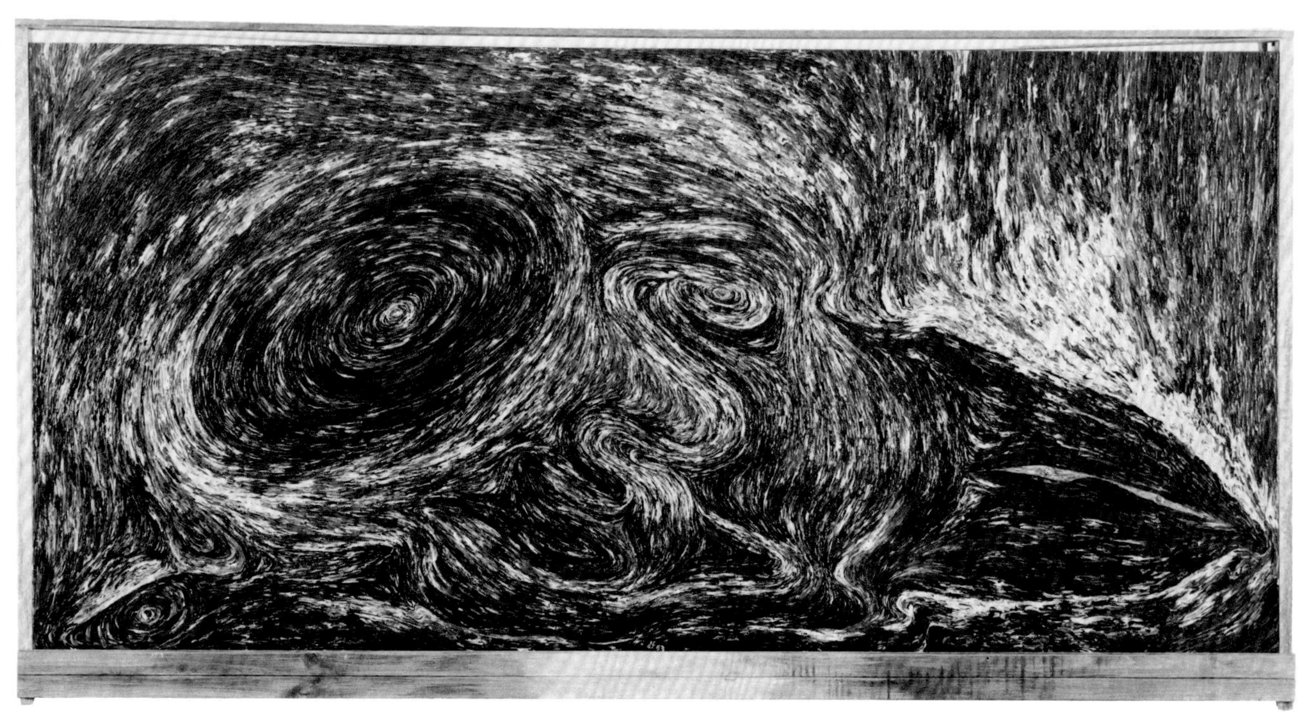

12 *Knowing the secret trick of a one word title. Self portrait with shadow.* 1983
Acrylic on canvas, 74¾ x 143¾″ (190 x 365 cm.)
Courtesy Roslyn Oxley9, Sydney

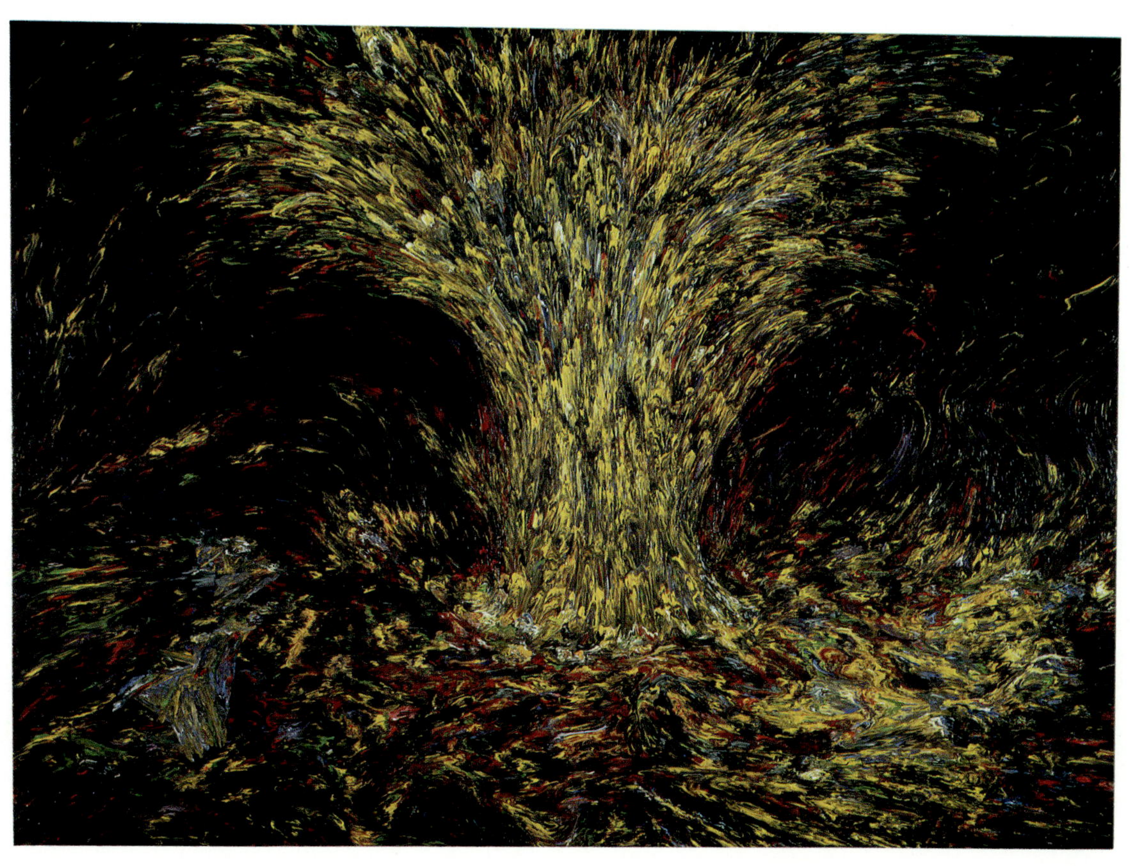

13 | *The sea and the sore eye.* 1984
Acrylic on canvas, 70⅞ x 94½″ (180 x 240 cm.)
Private collection, Milan

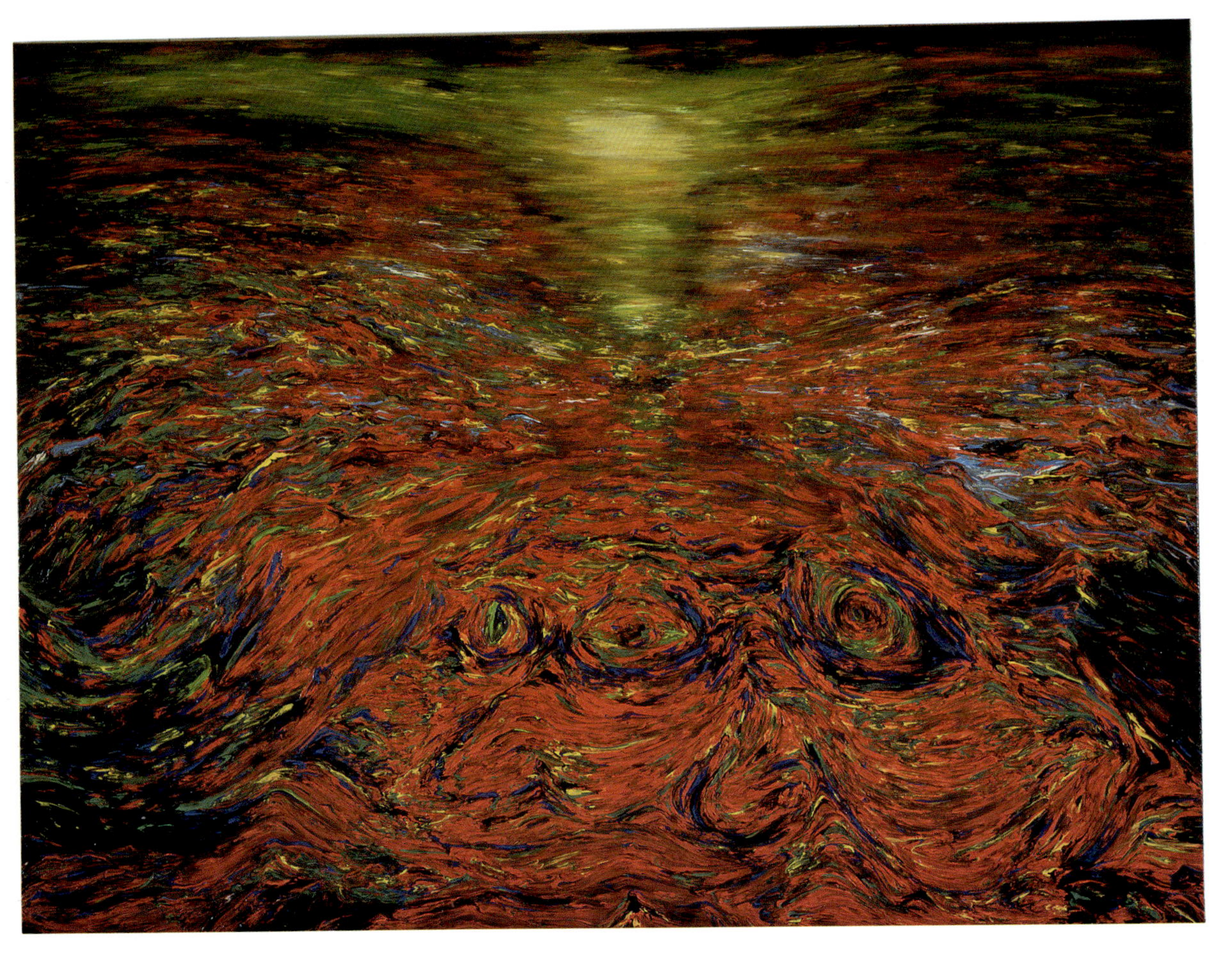

14 | *The wake.* 1984
Acrylic on canvas, 78¾ x 102⅜″ (200 x 260 cm.)
Courtesy Roslyn Oxley9, Sydney; Studio d'Arte
Cannaviello, Milan; Monique Knowlton Gallery,
New York

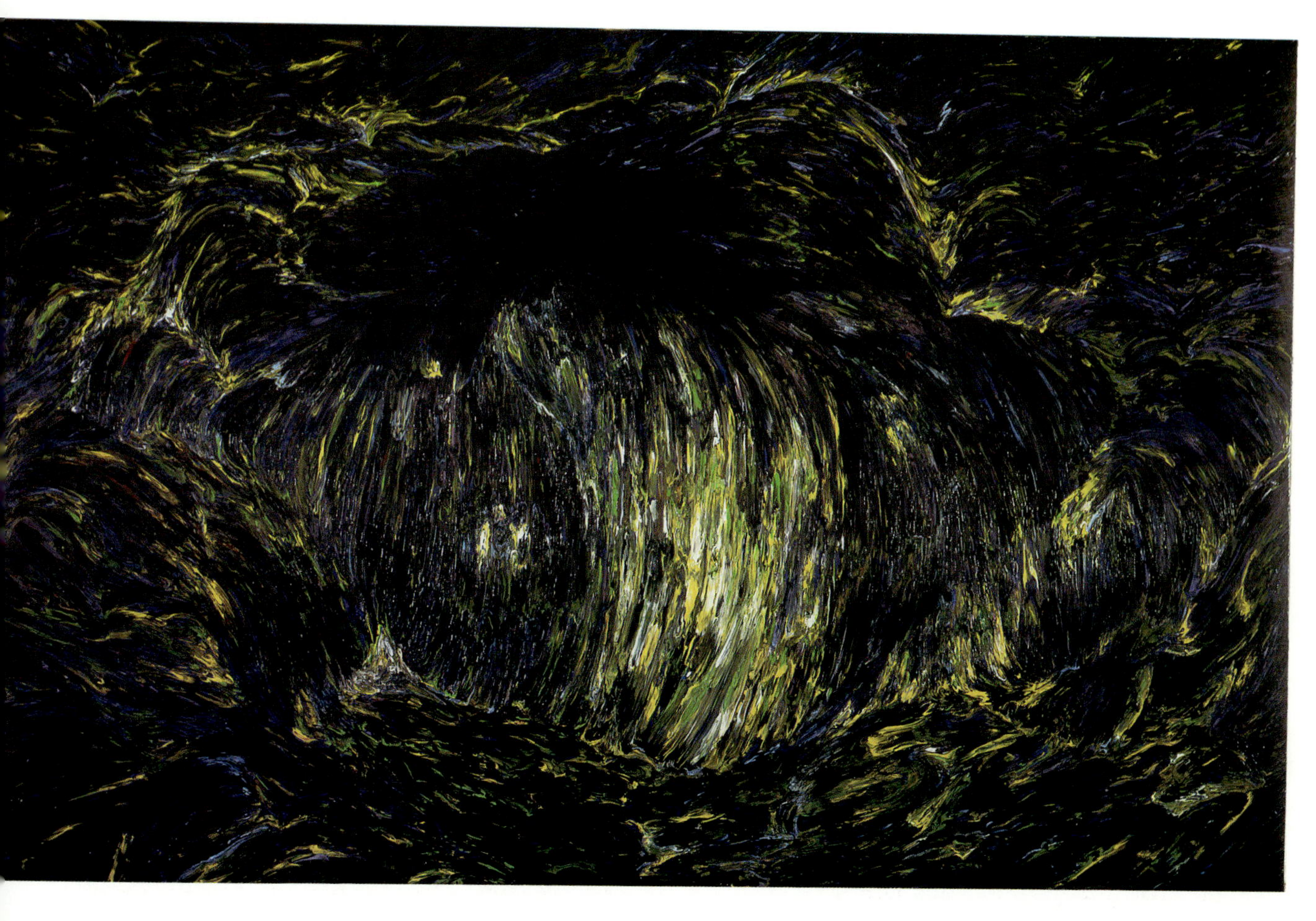

15 *The fall of the head of the peasant girl.* 1984
Acrylic on canvas, 78¾ x 118⅛″ (200 x 300 cm.)
Courtesy Roslyn Oxley9, Sydney; Studio d'Arte
Cannaviello, Milan; Monique Knowlton Gallery,
New York

BILL HENSON

Born in Melbourne, 1955

Prahran College of Advanced Education, Melbourne, 1973-75

Travels in Eastern Europe, including Warsaw, Prague, East Berlin and Dresden, 1979

Victorian College of the Arts, Melbourne, 1983

Guest lecturer, Photography Studies College and Victoria College, Melbourne, 1983

Travels in Europe and United States, 1984

Guest lecturer, Tasmanian College of Advanced Education, Hobart, 1984

Lives in Melbourne

Selected Group Exhibitions

Ewing Gallery, University of Melbourne, *Graduating Photography*, July 1974

Glenville Gallery, Perth, *The Nude*, opened May 1978. Traveled to Susan Gillespie Gallery, Canberra; Church Street Photographic Centre, Melbourne, 1978

The Photographers' Gallery, Melbourne, *New Australian Work*, September 1978

Australian Embassy, Paris, *Aspects of the Philip Morris Collection: Four Australian Photographers*, July-September 1980. Traveled in Australia. Catalogue with text by Anne-Marie Willis

Australian National University, Canberra, *Photography —The Last Ten Years* (organized by Australian National Gallery, Canberra), July-October 1980

Art Gallery of New South Wales, Sydney, *Australian Perspecta 1981: A biennial survey of contemporary Australian art*, May-June 1981. Catalogue with text by Bernice Murphy

Nantes Regional Gallery, France, *Scène, Séquence, Séries* (organized by Bibliothèque Nationale, Paris, and Musée des Beaux-Arts de Nantes), October-November 1981. Catalogue with texts by Jacques Py and Bernard-Xavier Vailhen

Art Gallery of New South Wales, Sydney, *Biennale of Sydney: Vision in Disbelief,* April-May 1982. Catalogue with texts by Elwyn Lynn and William Wright

James Harvey Gallery, Sydney, *Male*, July 1982

Tasmanian School of Art Gallery, University of Tasmania, Hobart, *Sexual Imagery in Art,* September 1982. Checklist with text by A. Dunstone

Galerie Jurka in association with Galerie Biederberg-Mueller and Galerie Wetering, Amsterdam, *Australian Artists in Amsterdam*, October 1983

Art Gallery of New South Wales, Sydney, *C.S.R. Photography Project*, October 1983. Catalogue with text by Christine Godden

Australian National Gallery, Canberra, *A Decade of Australian Photography, 1972-1982*, October 1983-January 1984. Catalogue with text by Ian North

ARC/Musée d'Art Moderne de la Ville de Paris, *D'un autre continent: l'Australie. Le rêve et le réel*, October 4-December 4, 1983. Catalogue with texts by Suzanne Pagé and Léon Paroissien

Sydney Opera House Exhibition Hall, *C.S.R. Photography Project: Selected Works*, March-April 1984

Selected One-Man Exhibitions

National Gallery of Victoria, Melbourne, *Of Tender Years*, July-August 1975. Checklist with text by Jennie Boddington

Church Street Photographic Centre, Melbourne, August 1978; February 1980

Australian Centre for Photography, Sydney, October 1979

Photographers' Gallery, London, *Bill Henson Photographs*, November 1981. Catalogue

The Developed Image Gallery, Adelaide, *Bill Henson: Untitled Series 1977*, February-March 1982

North Hobart Photographic Gallery, Hobart, July 1982

Cockatoo Gallery, Launceston, *Bill Henson Photographs*, May 1984. Checklist

Burnie Art Gallery, *Bill Henson Photographs*, September 1984

Storey Hall, Royal Melbourne Institute of Technology, 1984

Selected Bibliography

Laurence Le Guay, ed., *Australian Photography: A Contemporary View*, Sydney, 1974, pp. 20-22

Tony Perry, "Works both progressive and negative," *The Age*, August 15, 1978, p. 2

James Mollison, ed., *Australian Photographers: The Philip Morris Collection*, collection cat., Melbourne, 1979, pp. 68, 103

Tony Perry, "Mood Framed in Chaos," *The Age*, February 23, 1980, p. 2

"Pictures on the Move," *The Sun*, July 12, 1980, pp. 10-11

Christine Godden, "Photography and the Australian Art Scene," *Art and Australia,* vol. 18, Summer 1980, pp. 175-182

"From a Sequence," *London Magazine*, vol. 20, November-December 1980, pp. 59-62

Edward Brash, ed., *Photography Year: 1980 Edition*, Alexandria, Virginia, 1980, p. 57

Alwynne Mackie, *Bill Henson and the Possibilities of Photography*. Unpublished text, Australian National University, Canberra, 1980

Nancy Borlase, "Perspecta 81," *The Sydney Morning Herald*, May 30, 1981, p.47

Terry Smith, "The State of the Art," *The National Times*, June 1981, p. 43

Michel Muridsany, "Scène, Séquence, Séries," *Le Figaro*, October 7, 1981, p. 27

Janine Burke, "Art for the End of the World," *Meanjin*, vol. 40, October 1981, pp. 381, 383-388

Caroline Caugolie, "Scène, Séquence, Séries," *Libération*, November 2, 1981, p. 24

Geoff Strong, "A Dark Age Behind the Camera," *The Age*, November 30, 1981, p. 10

Alain Fleig, "Scène, Séquence, Séries," *Caval*, November 1981

Gael Newton, *Project 38: Re-constructed Vision: Contemporary work with photography*, exh. cat., Sydney, 1981

Bernice Murphy, "Flash Art Australia: Bill Henson," *Flash Art*, December 1981-January 1982, p. 61

Craig McGregor and Christine Godden, "The Photographers—The New Subjectivism," *The National Times,* March 21, 1982, pp. 22-23

Neville Weston, "An Interesting Link," *Adelaide Advertiser*, March 1982, p. 7

Arthur McIntyre, "The Biennale of Sydney," *The Age*, April 14, 1982, p. 10

Mick Carter, "Love in a Cold Climate," *Hobart Mercury*, July 9, 1982, p. 7

Virginia Hollister, "Pain and Pleasure—4th Biennale of Sydney," *Artlink*, vol. 2, July-August 1982, p. 4

Lutz Presser, "Sexual Imagery—A Step Towards Liberation," *Hobart Mercury*, September 18, 1982, p. 10

Gael Newton, "Photography: Towards a Dialogue with other media," *Australian Art Review*, October 1982, pp. 42, 44-46, 86, 128

Elwyn Lynn, "4th Biennale of Sydney," *Art International*, vol. XXV, no. 7-8, 1982, p. 42

James Mollison and Laura Murray, eds., *Australian National Gallery: An Introduction*, Canberra, 1982, pp. 143, 146

Helen Innes, "Melbourne Galleries," *Photo File*, Sydney, June 1983, p. 14

Le Pechoux, ed., *Australian Photography Yearbook,* Melbourne, 1983, pp. 128-129

Bernice Murphy and Janet Parfenovics, "1981 Update," *Australian Perspecta 1983: A biennial survey of contemporary Australian art,* exh. cat., Sydney, 1983, p. 120

Jennifer Phipps, "Entre deux Mondes—Australians in Paris," *The Age Monthly Review*, vol. 3, January 1984, p. 12

Mark Hinderaker, "Production spied through camera's eye," *The Sydney Morning Herald*, March 31, 1984, p. 14

Ian McLean, "Work Surrounds the Viewer," *Launceston Examiner,* May 9, 1984, p. 40

Ann Scott Young, "Bill Henson," *Launceston Examiner,* May 9, 1984, p. 40

"Bill Henson Photographs," *Tension,* no. 4, July 1984

"Bill Henson Photographs," *London Magazine*, vol. 24, July-August 1984

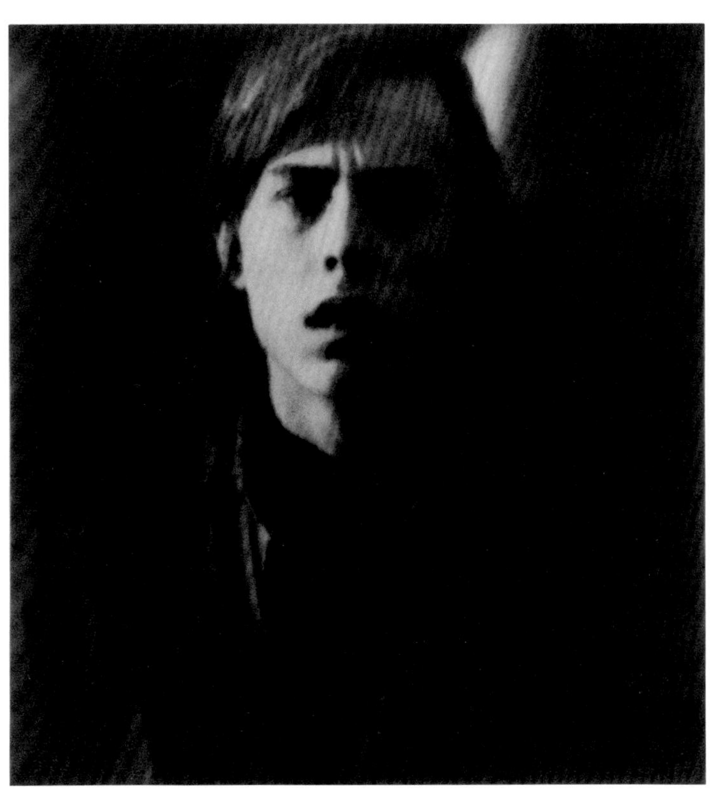

16 | Image from *Untitled 1980/82*. 1980-82
Gelatin silver print, image 17 x 15¼″
(43 x 38.9 cm.)
Collection of the artist

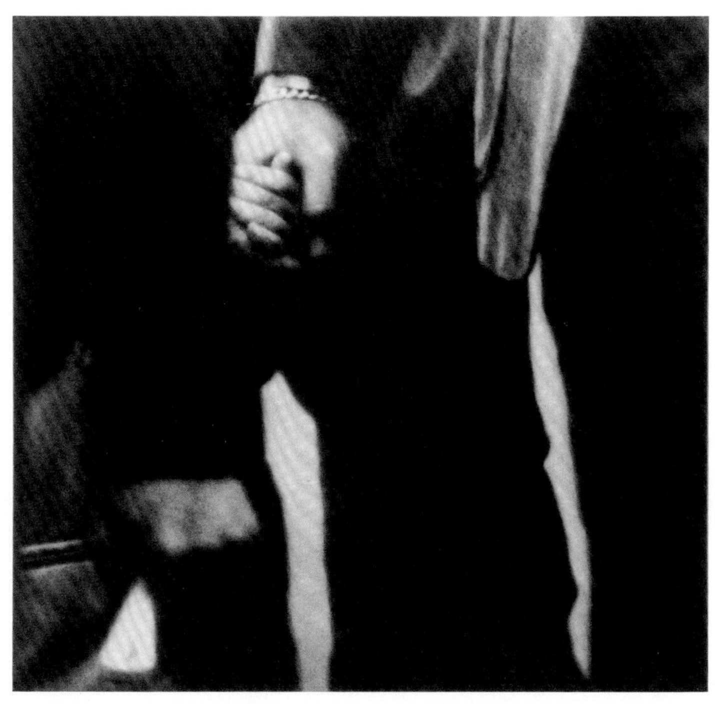

17 | Image from *Untitled 1980/82*. 1980-82
Gelatin silver print, image 14⅞ x 15¼″
(37.9 x 38.9 cm.)
Collection of the artist

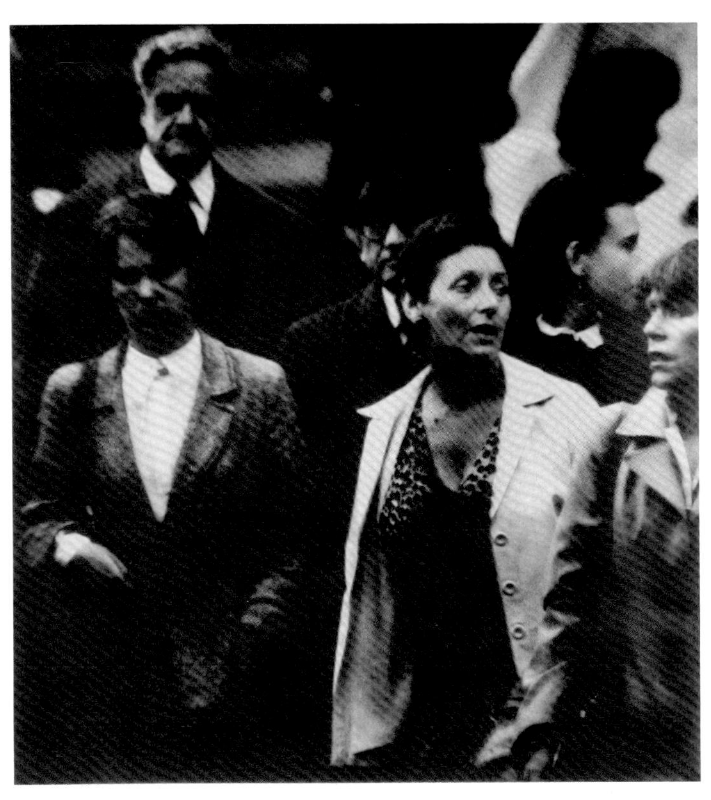

18 Image from *Untitled 1980/82*. 1980-82
Gelatin silver print, image 17 x 15¼″
(43 x 38.9 cm.)
Collection of the artist

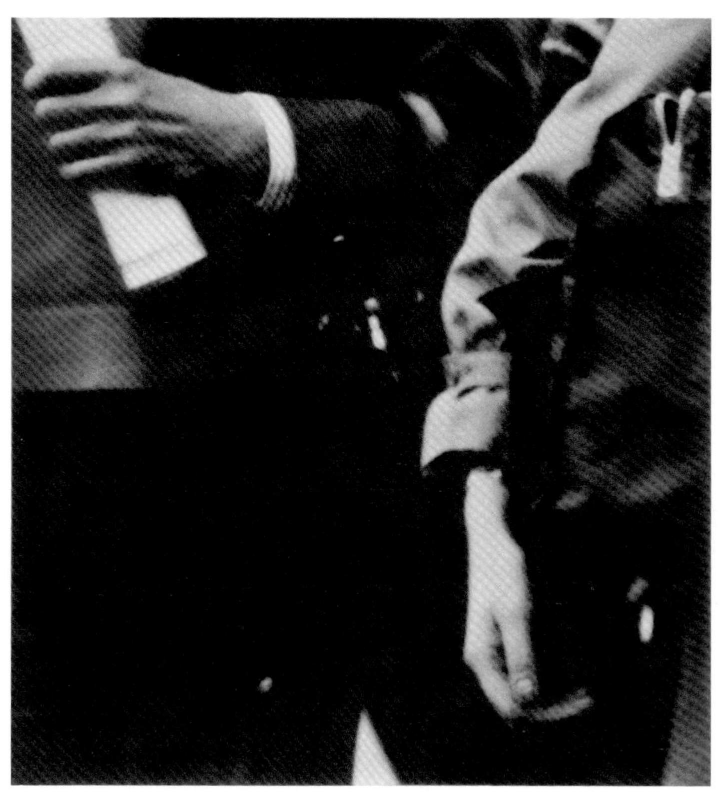

19 | Image from *Untitled 1980/82.* 1980-82
Gelatin silver print, image 17 x 15¼″
(43 x 38.9 cm.)
Collection of the artist

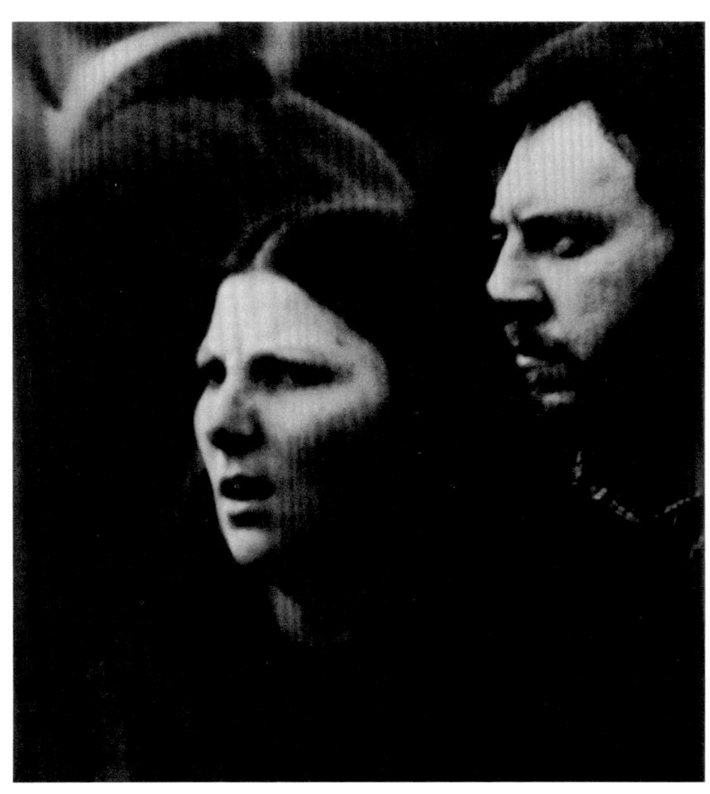

20 Image from *Untitled 1980/82.* 1980-82
Gelatin silver print, image 17 x 15¼″
(43 x 38.9 cm.)
Collection of the artist

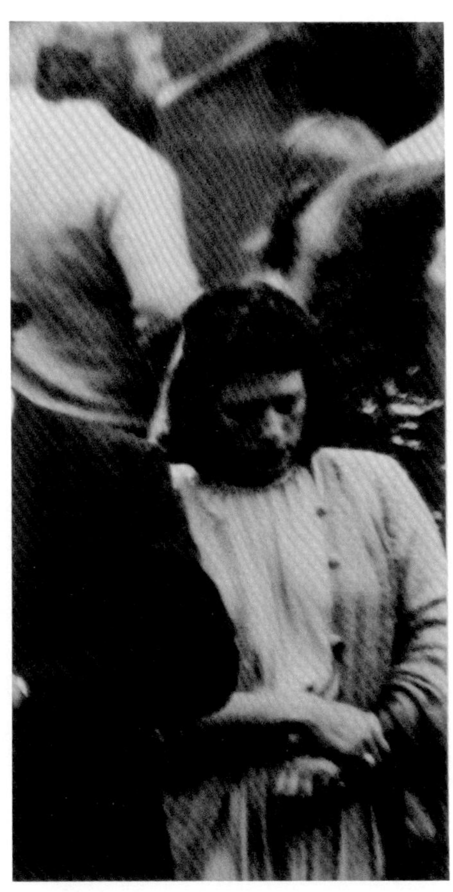

21 | Image from *Untitled 1980/82*. 1980-82
Gelatin silver print, image 19⅝ x 9⅞"
(49.8 x 25 cm.)
Collection of the artist

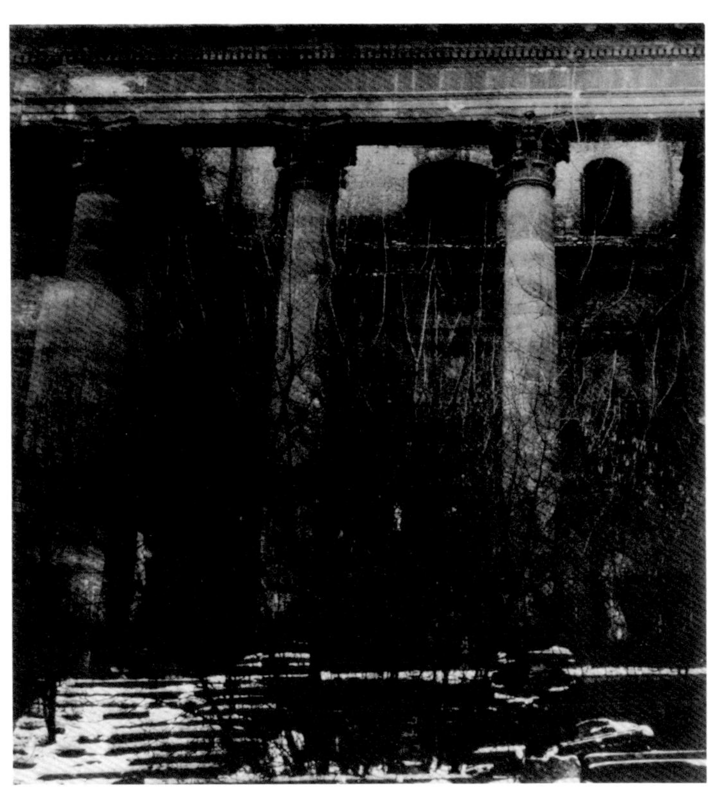

22 Image from *Untitled 1980/82*. 1980-82
Gelatin silver print, image 17 x 15¼″
(43 x 38.9 cm.)
Collection of the artist

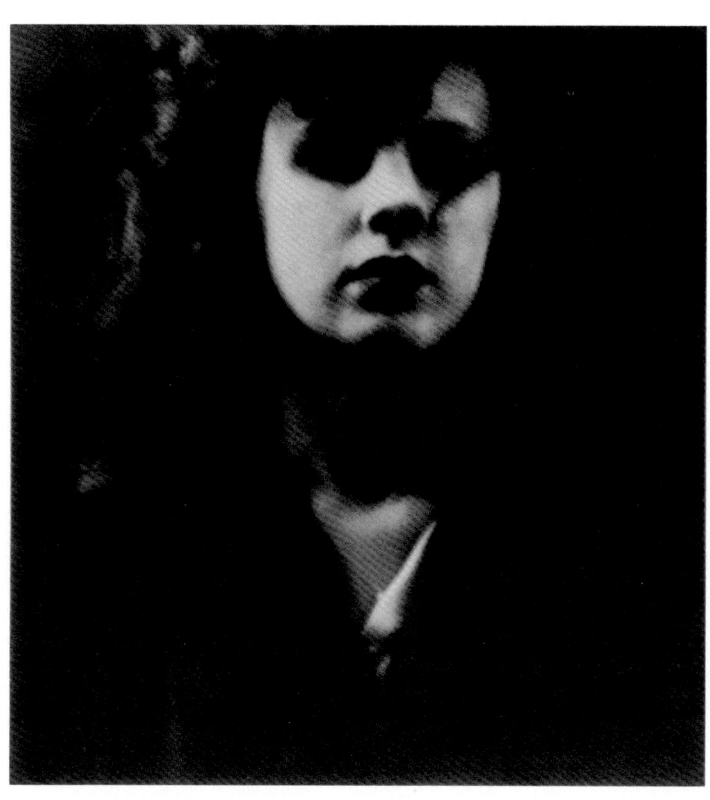

23 | Image from *Untitled 1980/82.* 1980-82
Gelatin silver print, image 17 x 15¼″
(43 x 38.9 cm.)
Collection of the artist

MANDY MARTIN

Born in Adelaide, 1952

Studies with Ruth Tuck, Adelaide, 1961-69

South Australia School of Art, Adelaide, 1972-75

Visual Arts Board Grant, 1977

Lecturer, Printmaking Workshop, Canberra School of Art, 1978-present

Travels in Europe and United States, 1979-80; Europe, 1982

John McCaughey Memorial Art Prize, National Gallery of Victoria, Melbourne, 1983

Artist in Residence, Institute of Modern Art, Brisbane, June-September 1984

Lives in Canberra

Selected Group Exhibitions

Royal South Australian Society of Arts Gallery, Adelaide, *Seven Young Artists*, February 1976

Hogarth Galleries, Sydney, *Women in Society, Parts I and II*, March 1976

University of Sydney, *Women's Fantasy and Reality*, June-July 1976

Progressive Art Movement exhibitions at Media Resource Centre, factories and supermarkets, Adelaide, *Women in Art*, 1976

Art Gallery of New South Wales, Sydney, *Project 18: Some recent art in Adelaide*, June-July 1977. Catalogue with text by Bernice Murphy

Experimental Art Foundation, Adelaide, *The Women's Show,* August 1977

Watters Gallery, Sydney, *Walls Sometimes Speak* (political posters), September 1977

George Paton Gallery, University of Melbourne, *Lost and Found—Objects and Images*, October 1978

Susan Gillespie Galleries, Canberra, *Works on Paper*, December 1978

Solander Gallery, Canberra, *Canberra School of Art Staff Exhibition*, May 1979

National Gallery of Victoria, Melbourne, *Selected Works from the Michell Endowment*, December 1979-March 1980

National Gallery of Victoria, Melbourne, *Survey 12: On Paper,* June-July 1980. Catalogue with text by Robert Lindsay and statement by the artist

Art Gallery of New South Wales, Sydney, *Australian Perspecta 1981: A biennial survey of contemporary Australian art*, May-June 1981. Catalogue with text by Bernice Murphy; statement by the artist reprinted from *Survey 12: On Paper*, exh. cat., 1980

Art Gallery of New South Wales, Sydney, *Some Australian Drawings 1880-1980*, May-June 1981

Art Gallery of South Australia, Adelaide, *Visions After Light: Art in South Australia 1836-1981*, June-August 1981

Art Gallery of South Australia, Adelaide, *Graven Images in the Promised Land,* June-August 1981. Catalogue with text by Alison Carroll

Royal South Australian Society of Arts Gallery, Adelaide, *Spectres of our Time*, August 1981. Checklist with text by Ron Radford

National Gallery of Victoria, Melbourne, *Contemporary Australian Prints since 1975*, August-September 1981

Visual Arts Board, Regional Development Program No. 9, Sydney, *From the Bottom to the Top,* opened December 1981. Catalogue. Traveled in Australia until July 1982

Canberra School of Art Gallery, *Canberra School of Art Staff Exhibition,* May-June 1982. Catalogue with text by Peter Haynes

Ivan Dougherty Gallery, Sydney, *Urban Images*, June-July 1982. Traveled to Wollongong City Gallery, New South Wales, August-September 1982

Institute of Modern Art, Brisbane, *Australian Screenprints 1982,* September 1982. Catalogue with text by Alison Carroll. Traveled in Australia

Art Gallery of New South Wales, Sydney, *Project 39: Women's Imprint*, October 1982. Checklist with text by Anna Waldman

ARC/Musée d'Art Moderne de la Ville de Paris, *XIIe Biennale de Paris*, October-November 1982

Newcastle Region Art Gallery, Newcastle, New South Wales, *Drawings in the Newcastle Region Art Gallery*, October-November 1982

National Gallery of Victoria, Melbourne, *The John McCaughey Memorial Art Prize*, February-March 1983

Newcastle Region Art Gallery, Newcastle, New South Wales, *Structures; for Urban Painters,* March-April 1983. Checklist with text by Andrew Sayers

Newcastle Region Art Gallery, Newcastle, New South Wales, *Mattara Invitation Art Purchase,* September 1983

National Gallery of Victoria, Melbourne, *Vox Pop,* December 1983-February 1984. Catalogue with text by Robert Lindsay

Art Gallery of South Australia, Adelaide, *Recent Australian Painting: A Survey 1970-1983*, December 1983-February 1984. Catalogue with text by Ron Radford

Art Gallery of Western Australia, Perth, *Form → Image← Sign: Biannual Survey of Contemporary Australian Art No. 3,* February-March 1984. Catalogue with text by Tony Bond

Powell Street Gallery, Melbourne, *Aspects of the Landscape.* Checklist with text by Barret Watson. Traveled to Geelong Art Gallery, Geelong. March-May 1984

Selected One-Woman Exhibitions

Hogarth Galleries, Sydney, *Screenprints,* June-July 1977

Bonython Galleries, Adelaide, September 1977

Abraxas Gallery, Canberra, October 1977

Hogarth Galleries, Sydney, August 1978

Contemporary Art Society, Adelaide, November 1978

Robin Gibson, Sydney, *Mixed Media Works on Paper*, August 1980

Solander Gallery, Canberra, December 1980

Powell Street Gallery, Melbourne, November-December 1981

Roslyn Oxley9, Sydney, *Mandy Martin: Paintings*, March 1983. Checklist with text by John Buckley

Powell Street Gallery, Melbourne, *Between the Ordinary and the Metaphysical*, July-August 1983

Institute of Modern Art, Brisbane, June-July 1984

Roslyn Oxley9, Sydney, October-November 1984

Selected Bibliography

By the Artist

"Different Strokes," *Art & Text,* vol. 14, Winter 1984, pp. 80-83

On the Artist

Heresies, January 1977, pp. 1, 95

Arthur McIntyre, "Mandy Martin—An Artist with Something to Say," *Aspect,* vol. 4, 1979, pp. 66-69

Maurice J. Symonds, C. Portley and R.E. Phillips, *The Visual Arts,* 2nd ed., Sydney, 1980, p. 188

Janine Burke, "Art for the End of the World," *Meanjin*, vol. 40, October 1981, pp. 375-388

Elwyn Lynn, "Letter from Australia," *Art International*, vol. XXV, May-June 1982, p. 78

"John McCaughey Memorial Art Prize 1983," *National Gallery of Victoria Bulletin*, April 1983, p. 10

Joanna Mendelssohn, "Jenny Watson and Mandy Martin—Roslyn Oxley9," *Art Network,* June 1983, pp. 17, 32, 65, 95

Bernice Murphy and Janet Parfenovics, "1981 Update," *Australian Perspecta 1983: A biennial survey of contemporary Australian art*, exh. cat., Sydney, 1983, p. 10

Sue Cramer, "Vox Pop," *Art & Text*, vol. 12-13, January 1984, p. 141

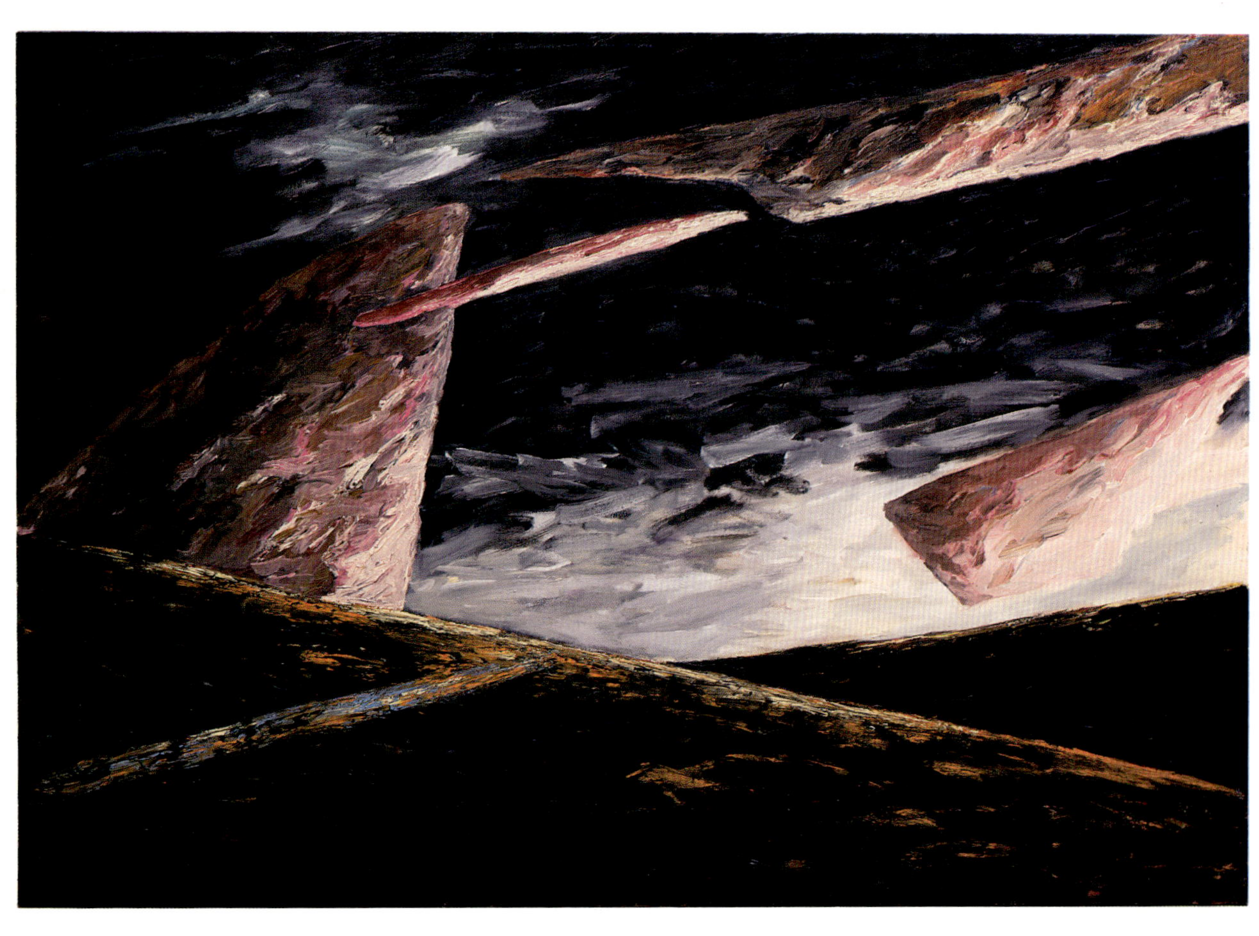

24 | *Spearhead.* 1983
Oil on canvas, 59¼ x 82¾″ (150.5 x 210 cm.)
Courtesy Powell Street Gallery, Melbourne

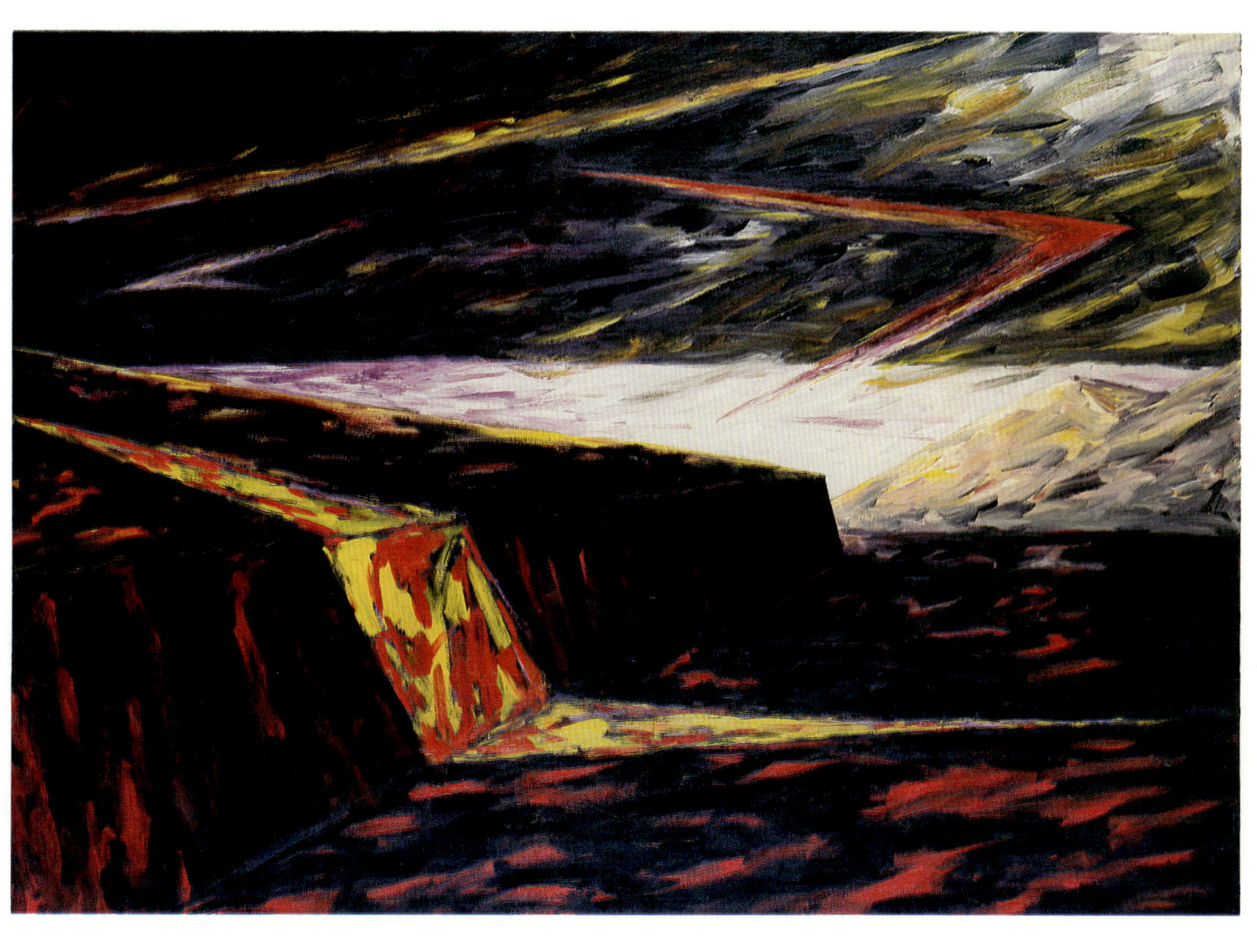

25 | *Great Shadow*. 1983
Oil on canvas, 60¼ x 82¾″ (153 x 210 cm.)
Courtesy Roslyn Oxley9, Sydney

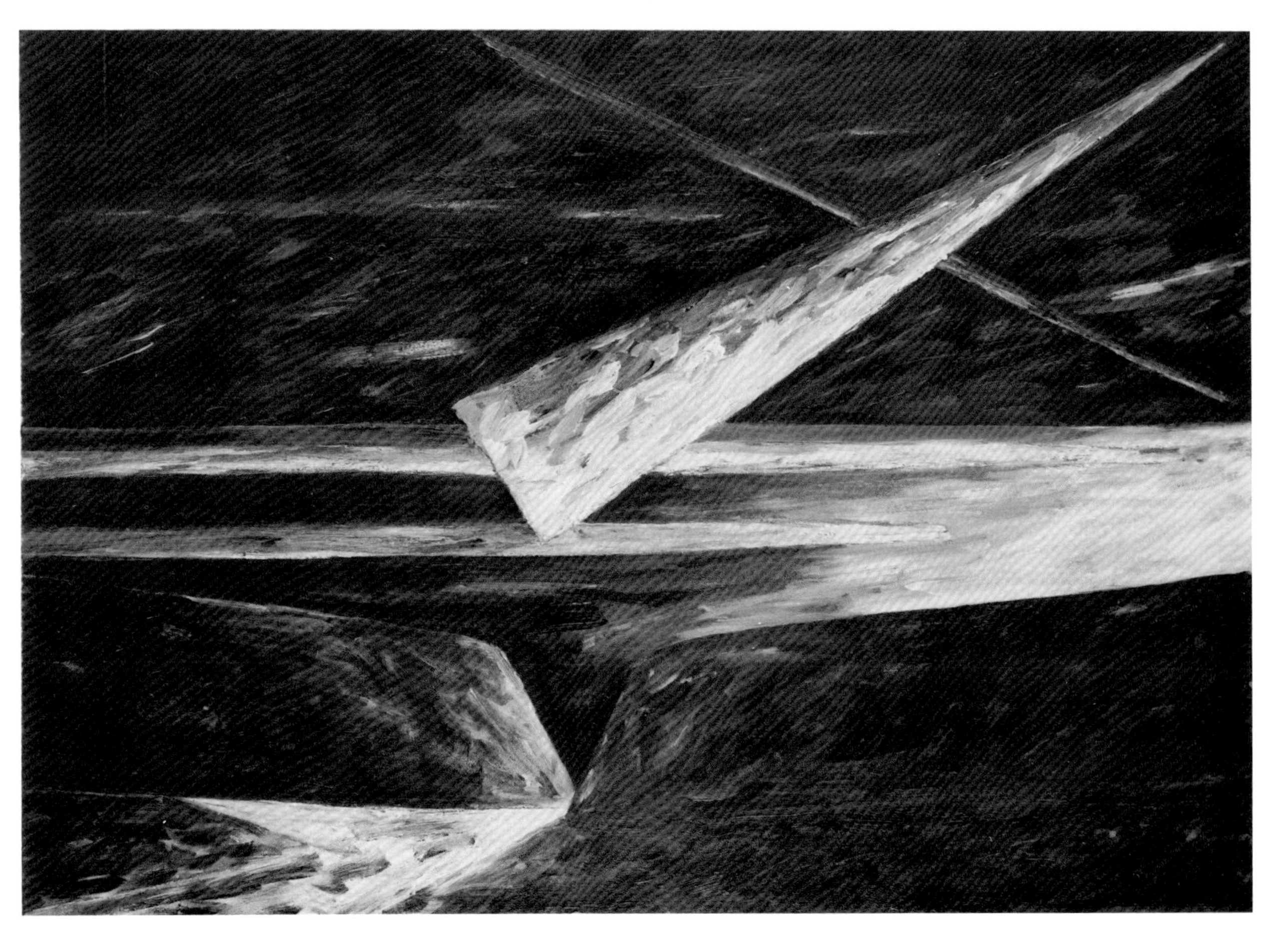

26   *Formation II.* 1983
Oil on canvas, 60 x 84″ (152.4 x 213.3 cm.)
Collection of the artist

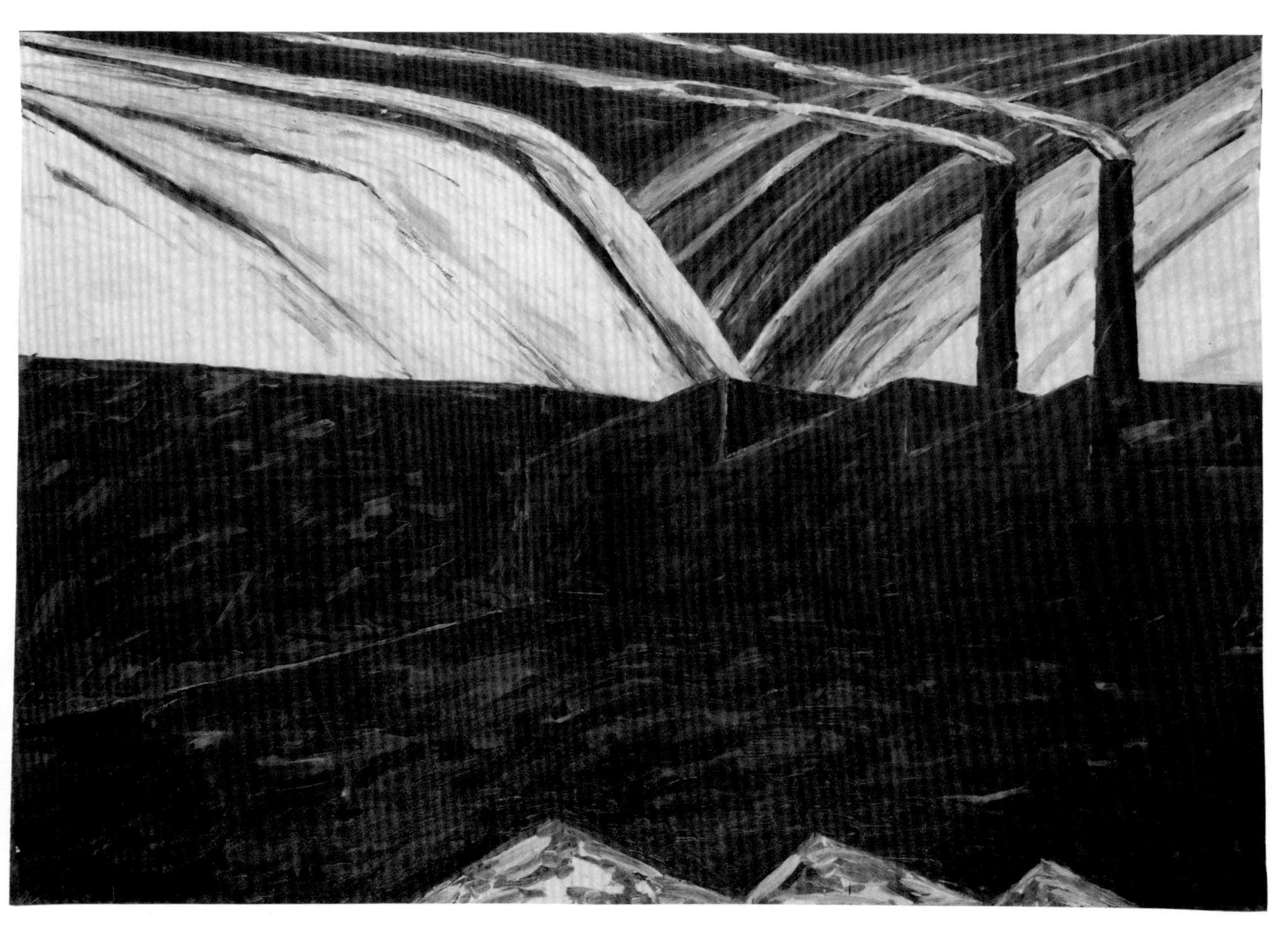

27 | *Barricade.* 1984
Oil on canvas, 68⅛ x 96″ (173 x 244 cm.)
Collection of the artist

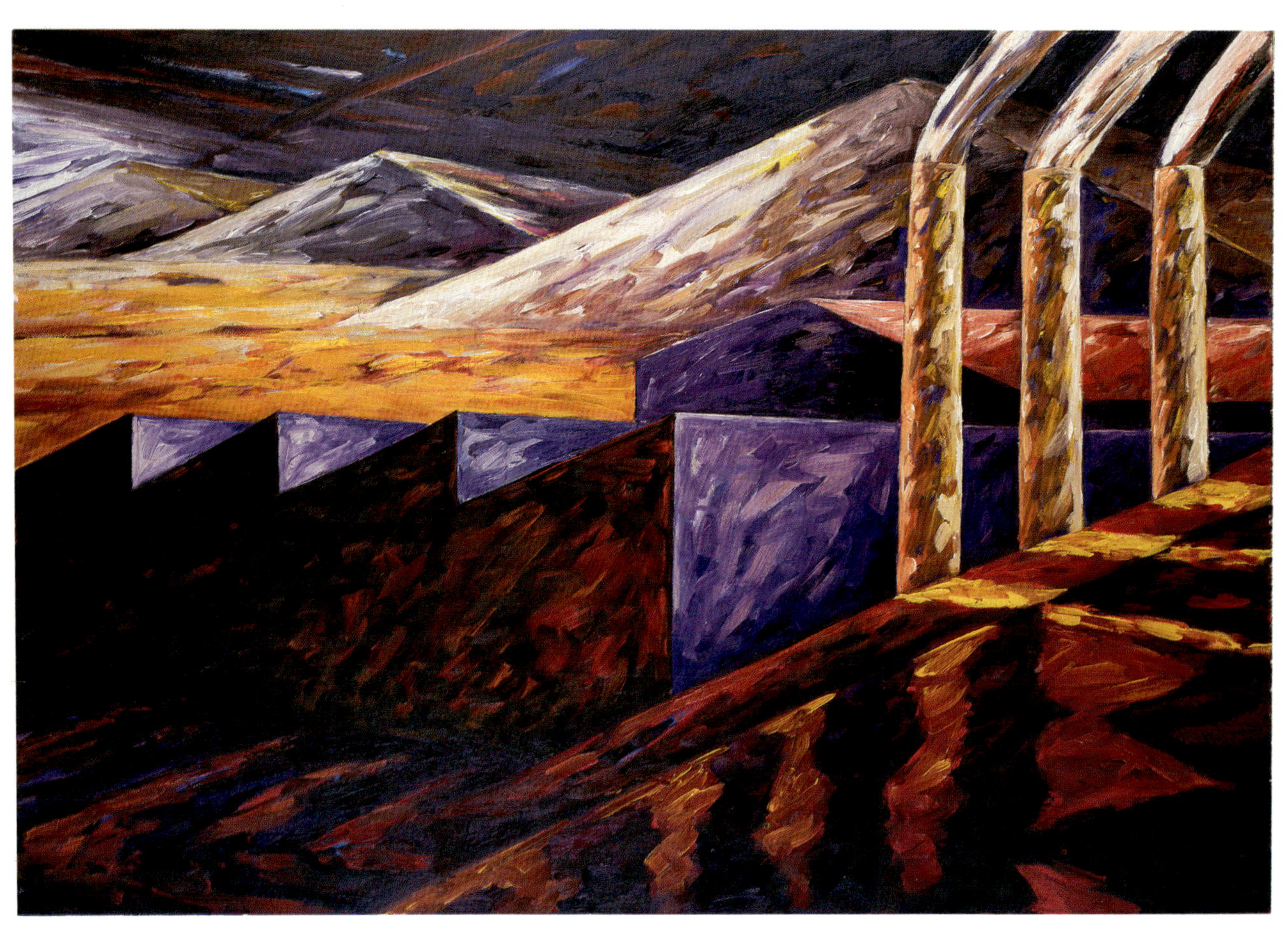

28 | *Phalanx.* 1984
Oil on canvas, 68⅛ x 96″ (173 x 244 cm.)
Collection of the artist

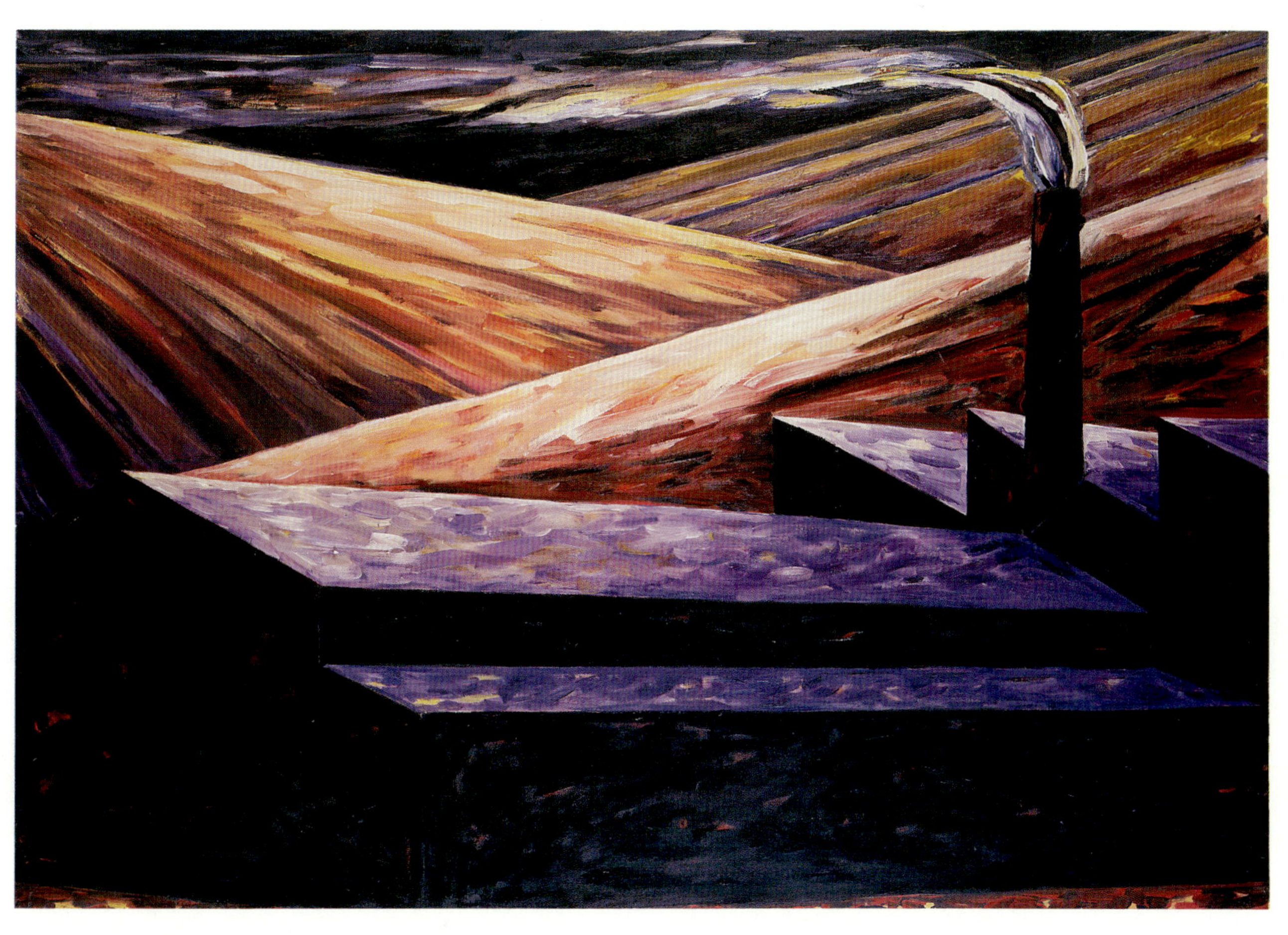

29 | *Interlock.* 1984
Oil on canvas, 68⅛ x 96″ (173 x 244 cm.)
Collection of the artist

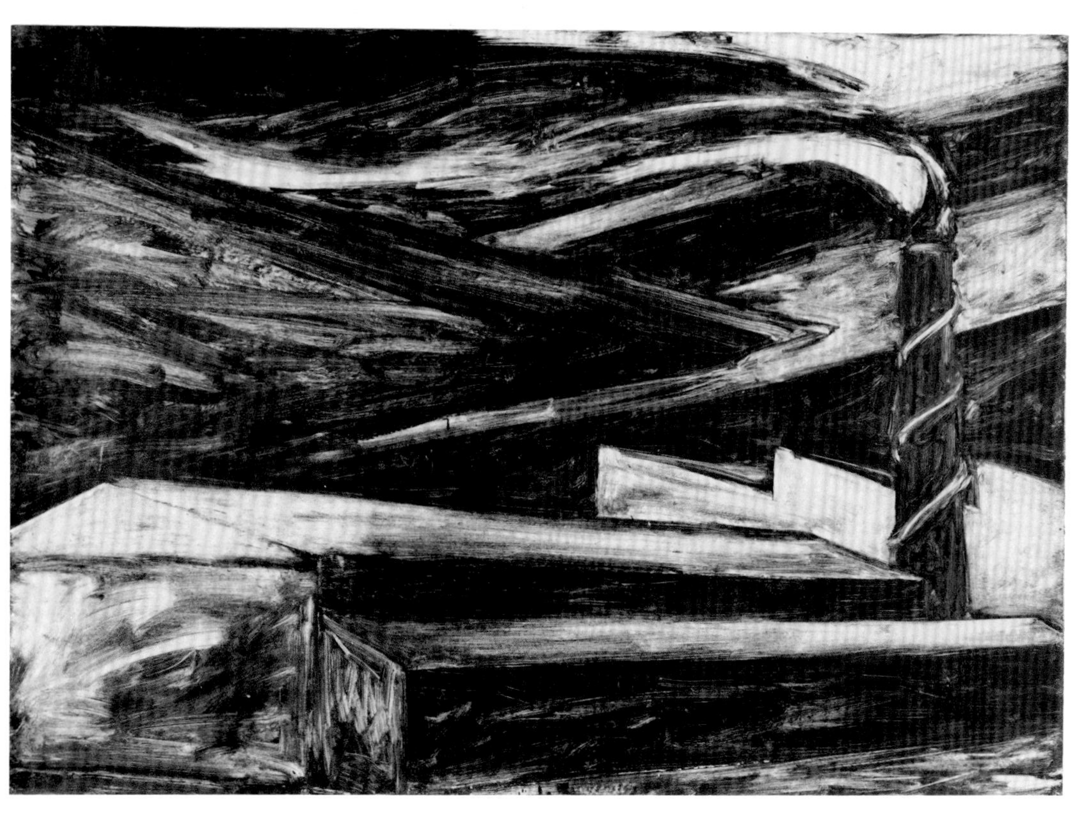

30 | *Interlock.* 1984
Oil on paper, 44⅞ x 61⅜″ (114 x 156 cm.)
Collection of the artist

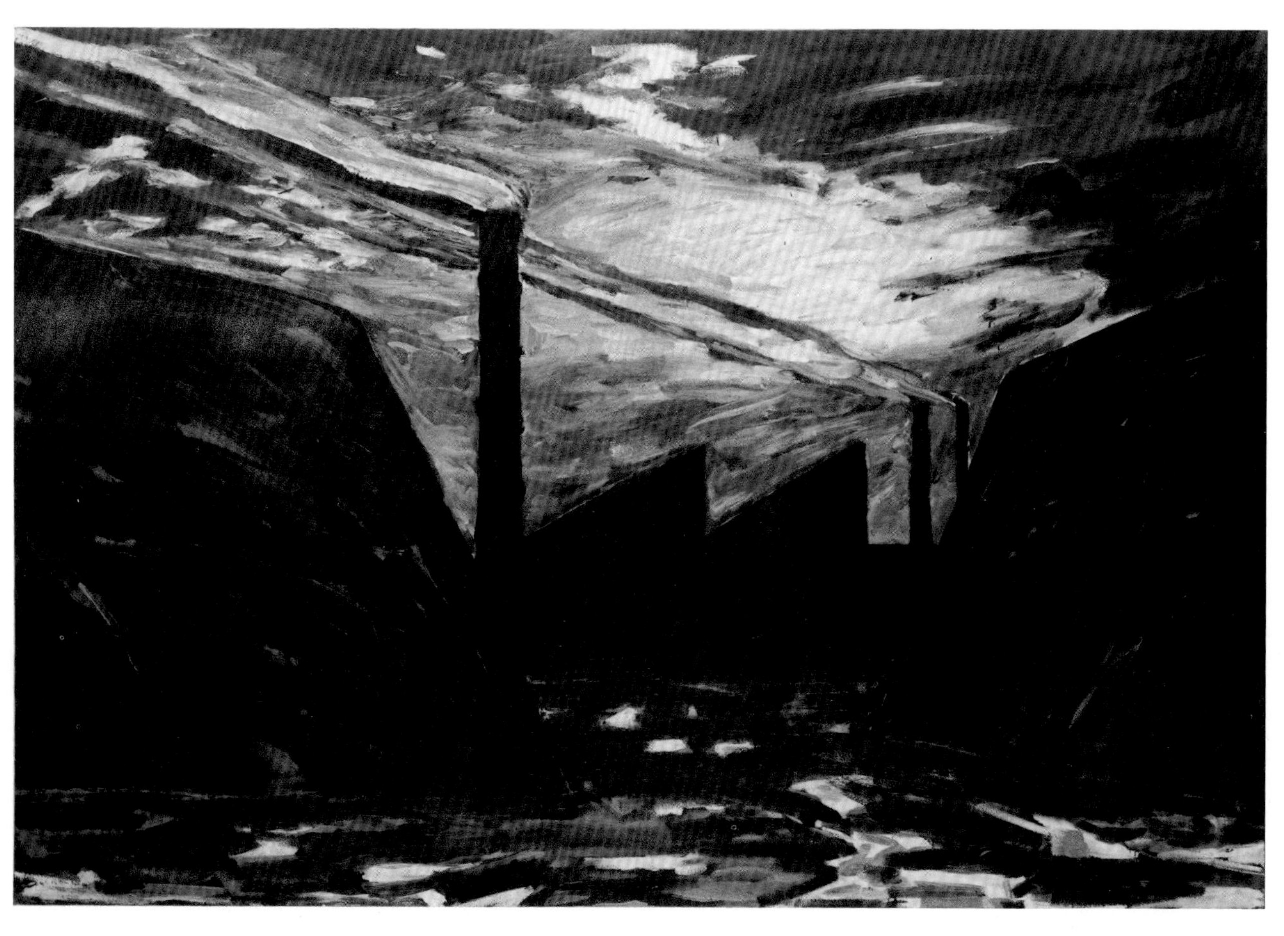

31 | *Break.* 1984
Oil on canvas, 68⅛ x 96″ (173 x 244 cm.)
Courtesy Roslyn Oxley9, Sydney

JAN MURRAY

Born in Ballarat, Victoria, 1957

Ballarat College of Advanced Education, 1976-78

Victorian College of the Arts, Melbourne, 1980-81

Part-time lecturer in painting at Victorian College of the Arts and Phillip Institute of Technology, Melbourne, 1983-present

Visual Arts Board Grant for twelve-month residency at Kunstlerhaus Bethanian, Berlin, 1984

Lives in Melbourne

Selected Group Exhibitions

Roslyn Oxley9, Sydney, *New Painting*, May-June 1982. Checklist with text by Memory Holloway

Monash University Gallery, Melbourne, *Young Melbourne Painters*, September-October 1982. Checklist with text by Memory Holloway

National Gallery of Victoria, Melbourne, *Selected Works from the Michell Endowment*, December 1982-January 1983

Victorian College of the Arts Gallery, Melbourne, *Keith and Elisabeth Murdoch Travelling Fellowship Exhibition*, February-March 1983

Art Gallery of New South Wales, Sydney, *Australian Perspecta 1983: A biennial survey of contemporary Australian art*, May 12-June 26, 1983. Catalogue with text by Bernice Murphy and Janet Parfenovics

ARC/Musée d'Art Moderne de la Ville de Paris, *D'un autre continent: l'Australie. Le rêve et le réel*, October 4-December 4, 1983. Catalogue with texts by Suzanne Pagé and Léon Paroissien

National Gallery of Victoria, Melbourne, *New Art: Selected Works from the Michell Endowment*, October 1983-February 1984

National Gallery of Victoria, Melbourne, *Vox Pop*, December 1983-February 1984. Catalogue with text by Robert Lindsay

Art Gallery of Western Australia, Perth, *Form → Image← Sign: Biannual Survey of Contemporary Australian Art No. 3*, February-March 1984. Catalogue with text by Tony Bond

One-Woman Exhibition

Roslyn Oxley9, Sydney, October-November 1983

Selected Bibliography

Terence Maloon, "Arts Review," *The Sydney Morning Herald,* May 22, 1982

Sandra McGrath, "Arts Review," *The Weekend Australian,* June 5-6, 1982

Bernice Murphy, "Recent Painting in Australia," *Flash Art*, January 1983, pp. 56-59

Suzanne Davies and Richard Dunn, "Grappling with Diversity: Australian Perspecta 1983," *Art Network,* June 1983, p. 14

Jill Montgomery, "AUSTRALIA—The French Discovery of 1983," *Art & Text*, January 1984, p. 15

Jennifer Phipps, "Entre deux Mondes—Australians in Paris," *The Age Monthly Review*, vol. 3, January 1984, p. 12

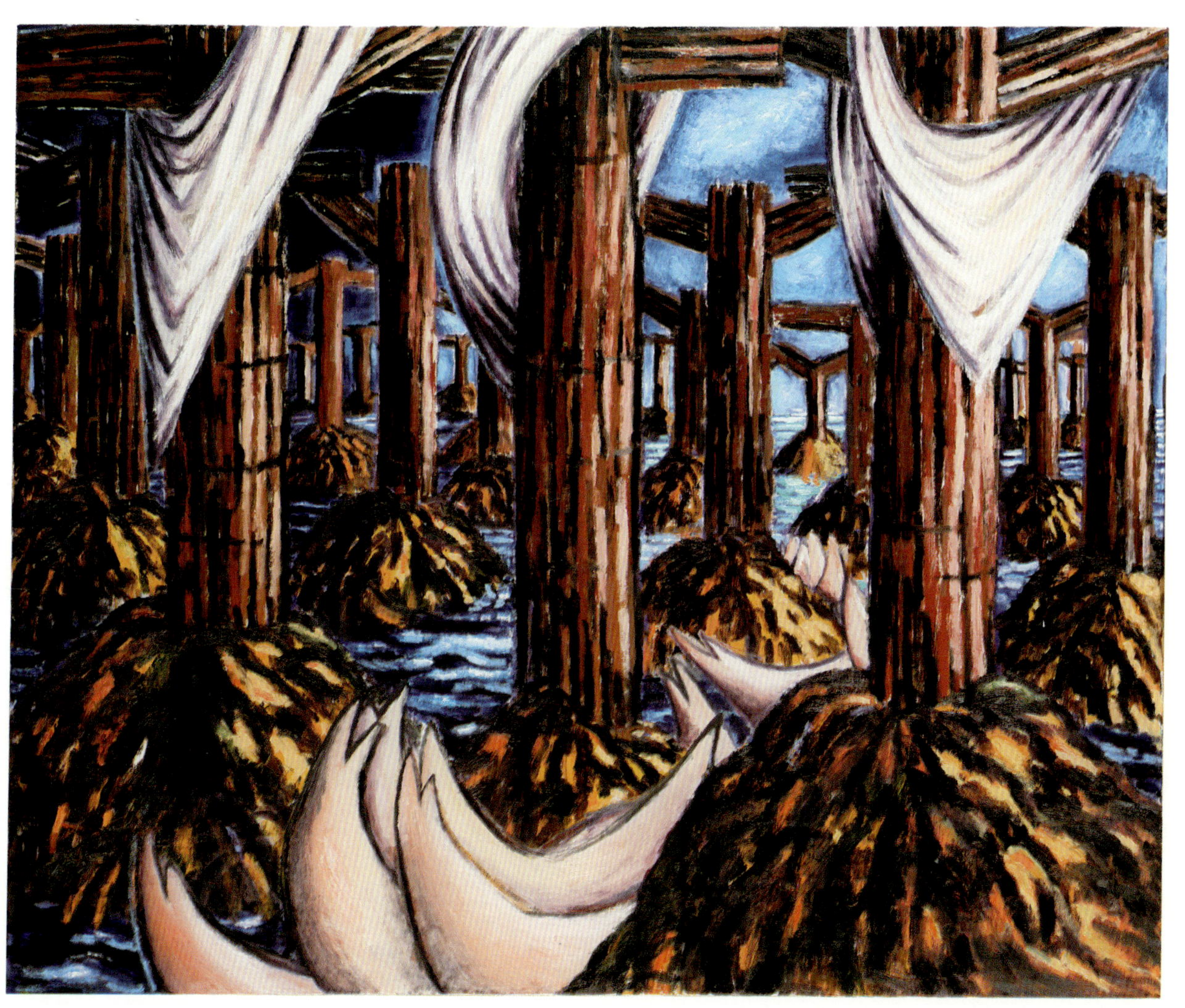

32 | *The Three Graces.* 1983
Oil on canvas, 65⅜ x 78″ (166 x 198 cm.)
Collection National Gallery of Victoria,
Melbourne; Michell Endowment, 1984

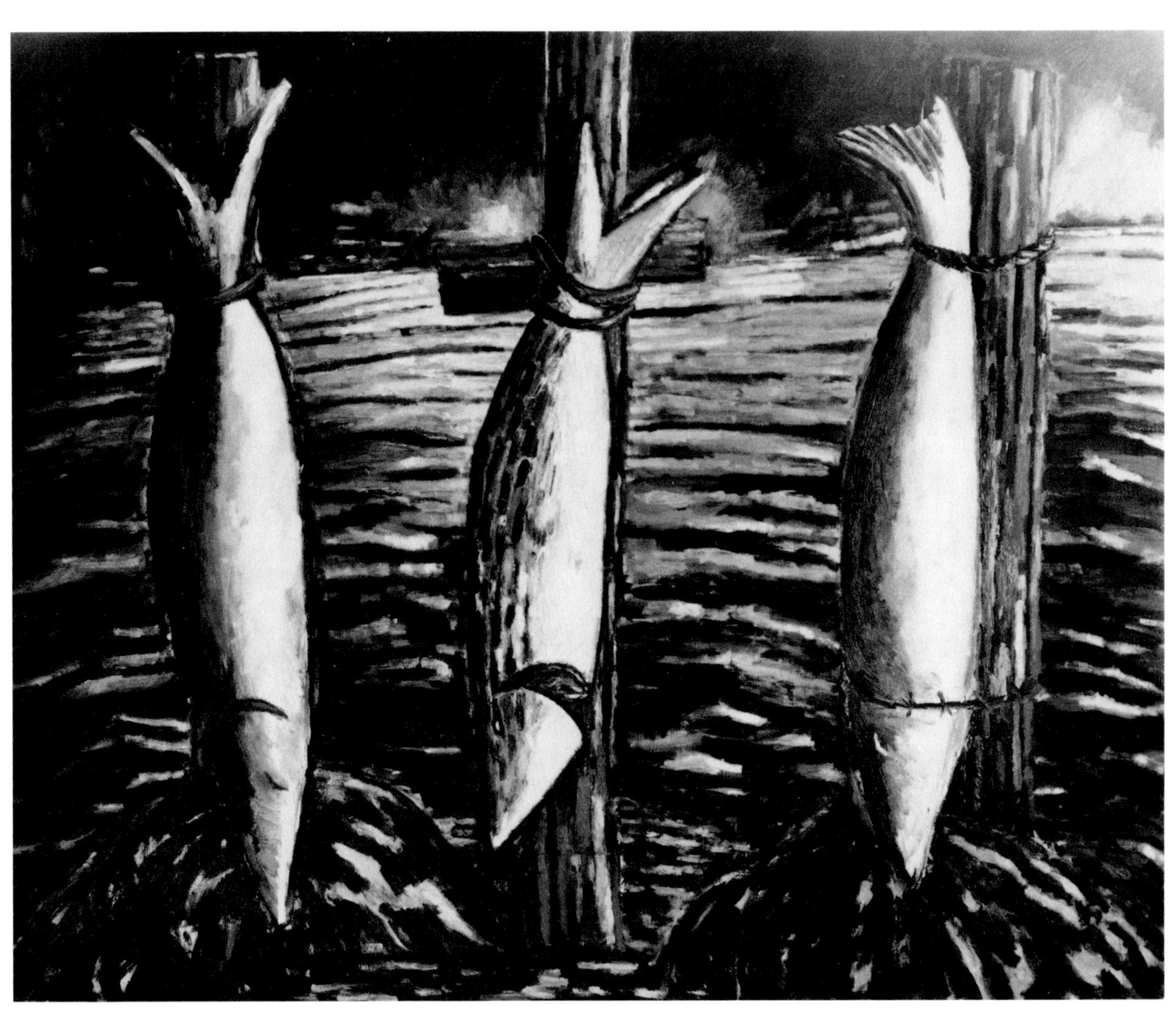

33 | *Three Fishes of the Sea.* 1983
Oil on canvas, 65⅝ x 78″ (166.5 x 198 cm.)
Private collection, Melbourne

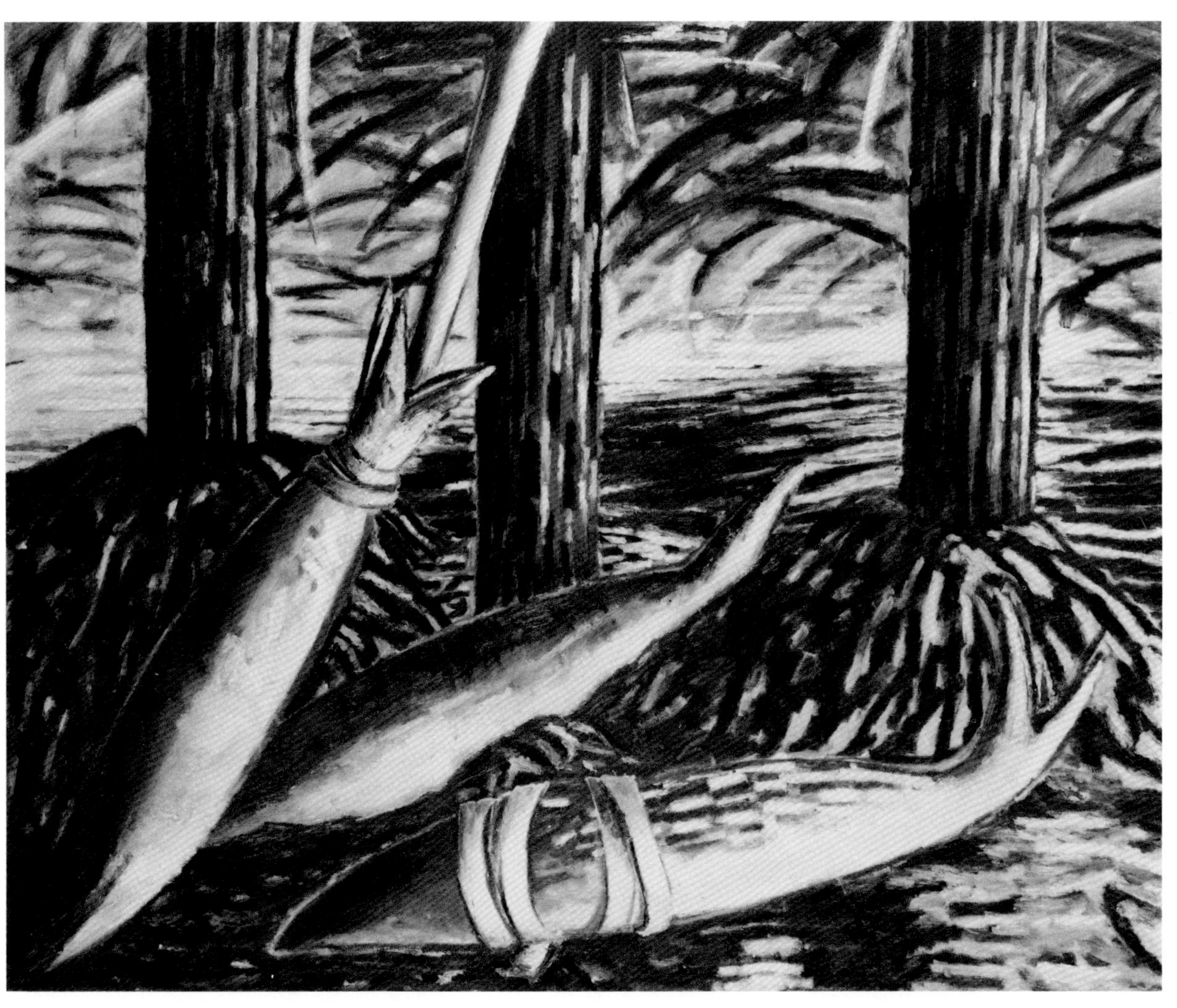

34 │ *The Descent.* 1983
Oil on canvas, 66⅛ x 78″ (168 x 198 cm.)
Courtesy Roslyn Oxley9, Sydney

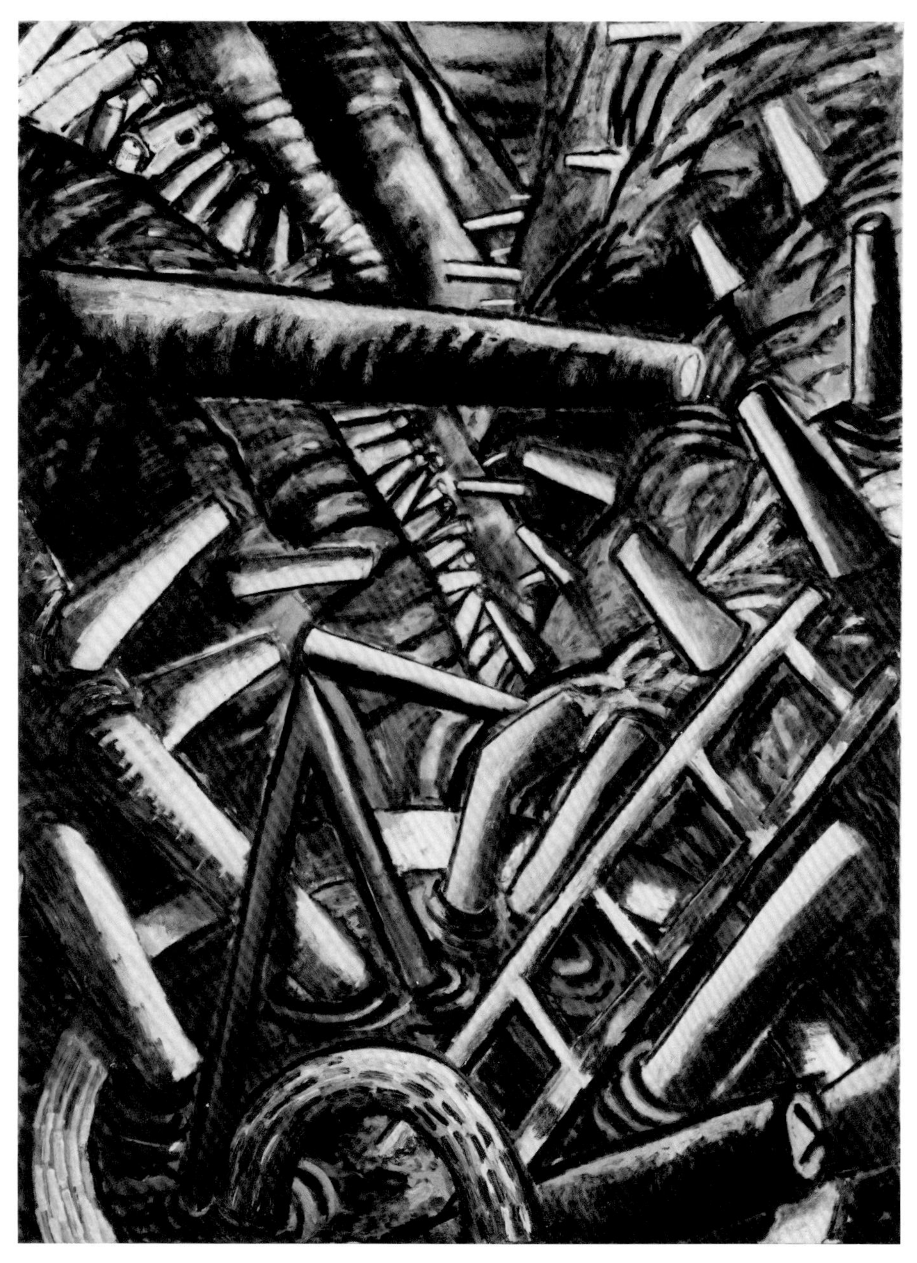

35 | *Engulfed II.* 1983
Oil on canvas, 83⅞ x 60¼″ (213 x 153 cm.)
Courtesy Roslyn Oxley9, Sydney

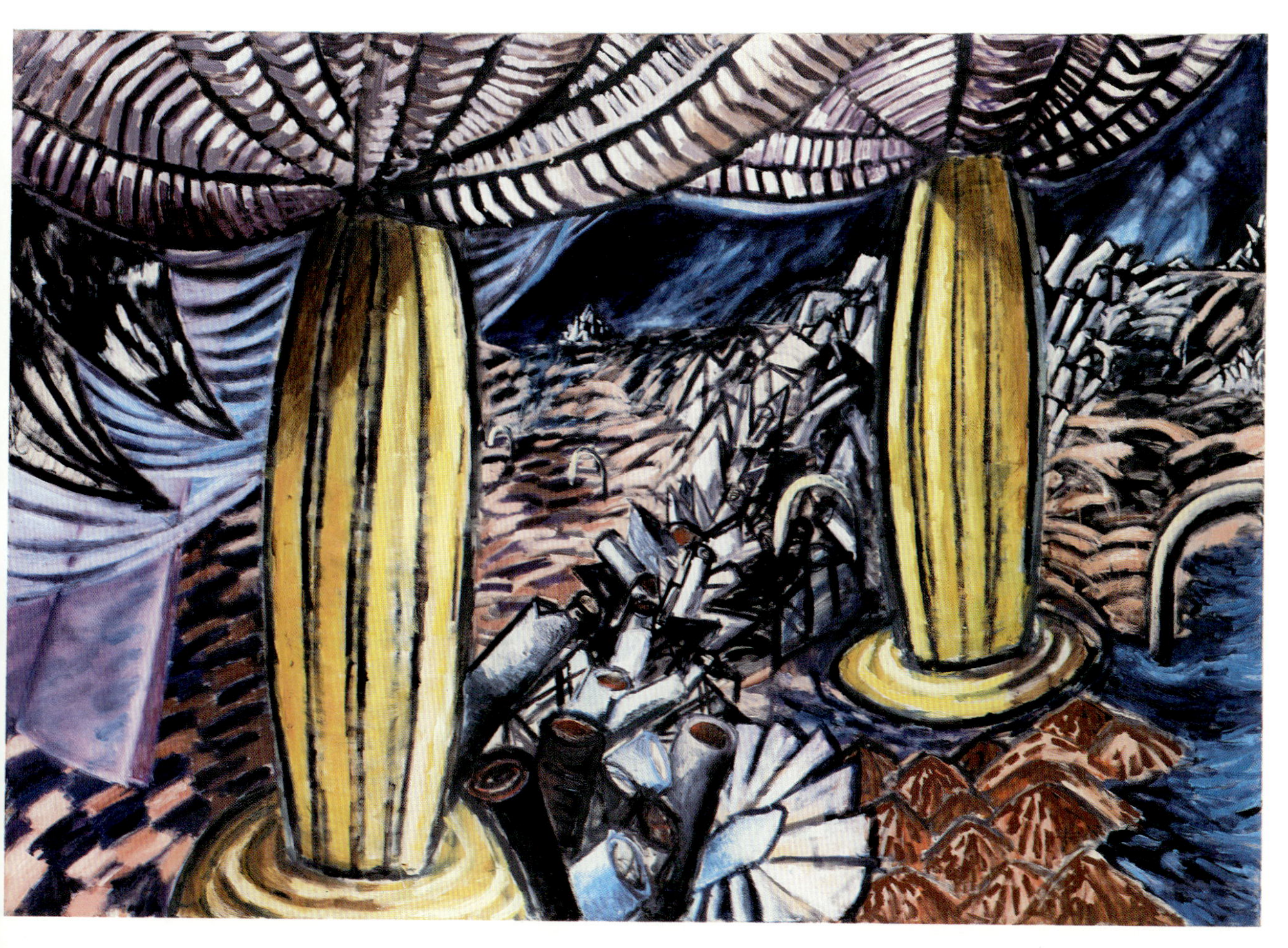

36 | *Lizard Landscape.* 1983
Oil on canvas, 60¼ x 83⅞″ (153 x 213 cm.)
Courtesy Roslyn Oxley9, Sydney

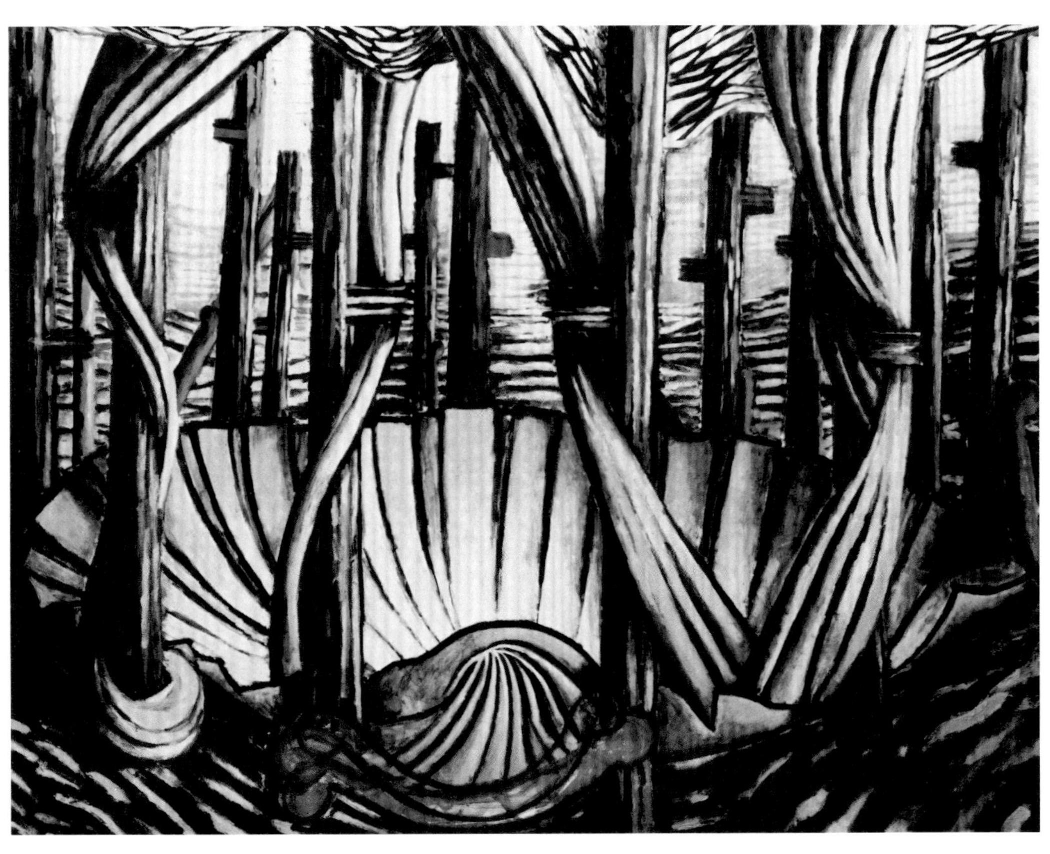

37 | *From Within the Shell.* 1983-84
Oil on linen, 65¾ x 83⅞″ (167 x 213 cm.)
Collection Phillip Institute of Technology,
Melbourne

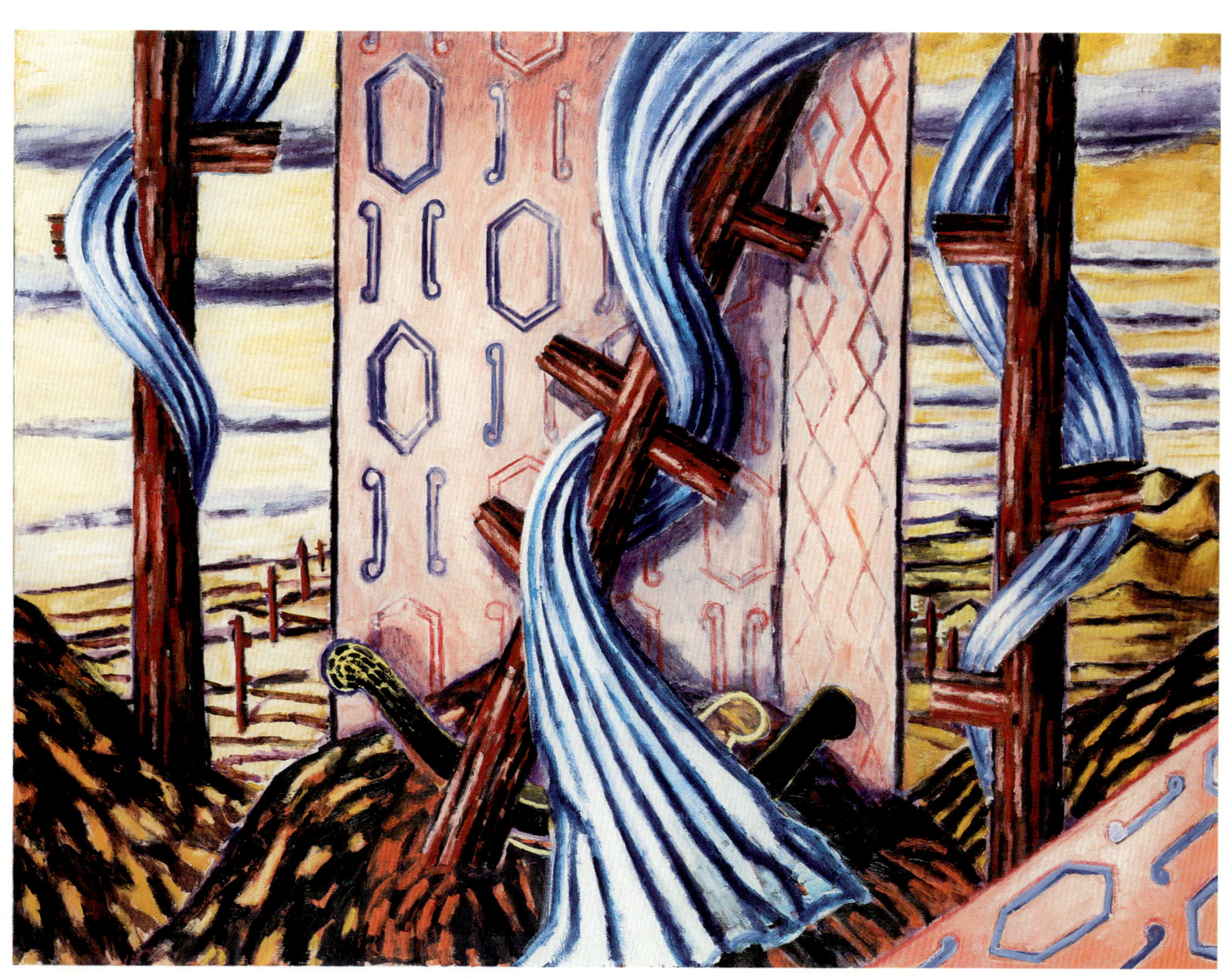

38 | *Screened Landscape.* 1983-84
Oil on canvas, 66⅛ x 84¼″ (168 x 214 cm.)
Courtesy Roslyn Oxley9, Sydney

JOHN NIXON

Born in Sydney, 1949

Moves to Melbourne, 1955

Preston Institute of Technology, Melbourne, 1967-68

National Gallery of Victoria Art School, Melbourne, Diploma of Art, 1969-70

State College of Victoria, Melbourne, Diploma of Education, 1973

Travels in Europe and United States, 1975-76

Lives in London, 1978

Travels in Europe, 1979

Founder and Director of Art Projects Annex Program, Melbourne, 1979

Founder and Director of Institute of Temporary Art, Melbourne, 1979

Founder and Director of Art Projects, Melbourne, 1979-84

Founder and Director of Q Space, Brisbane, 1980-81

Director of Institute of Modern Art, Brisbane, 1980-81

Founder and Director of V Space, Melbourne, 1980-83

Founder and Director of Office of the Institute of Artistic Culture, Brisbane, 1981

Founder and Director of I.T.A. (Institute of Temporary Art), Kassel, Paris, Düsseldorf, 1982

Guest curator, n-space, *Beacon No. 2*, Sydney, 1982

Guest curator (with Imants Tillers), n-space at The Temple of the Winds, *The Temple of The Winds*, Melbourne, 1982

Guest curator, University Gallery, University of Melbourne, *Apocalypse and Utopia*, 1984

Lives in Melbourne

Selected Group Exhibitions

National Gallery of Victoria, Melbourne, *Art and Language,* May 1975. Traveled to Art Gallery of South Australia, Adelaide, June-July

Australian National University Arts Centre, Canberra, *Act I: An Exhibition of performance and participatory art*, November 1978

Art Gallery of New South Wales, Sydney, *Biennale of Sydney: European Dialogue*, April-May 1979. Catalogue

Pitspace, Preston Institute of Technology, Melbourne, *Some Biennale Works and Information*, July-August 1979

Art Projects, Melbourne, *Group Show*, December 1979

Art Gallery of New South Wales, Sydney, *Archibald Prize (Rejected Entry)*, December 1979-January 1980; December 1981-January 1982

Art Projects, Melbourne, *The Archibald, Wynne and Sulman Prizes: Three Rejected Entries* (with Imants Tillers and Peter Tyndall), May 1981

n-space, Sydney, *The Beacon*, December 6, 1981

Art Projects, Melbourne, *PAINTING/PAINTING*, February 1982

Georges Gallery, Melbourne, *Georges Invitation Art Award*, May 1982

Kassel, West Germany, *Documenta 7*, June-September 1982. Catalogue with texts by Coosje van Bruggen, Germano Celant, Johannes Gachnang and Gerhard Storck

n-space at The Temple of the Winds, Melbourne, *The Temple of the Winds*, opened October 3, 1982

Art Gallery of New South Wales, Sydney, *Project 40: Australian Artists at Venice and Kassel*, February-March 1983. Catalogue with text by Bernice Murphy and statement by the artist

Exhibition Gallery, Monash University, Melbourne, *Masterpieces: Out of the Seventies*, March-May 1983. Checklist with text by Peter Cripps

University Gallery, University of Melbourne, *Tall Poppies: An exhibition of five pictures,* April-June 1983. Catalogue with text by Paul Taylor; reprinted as "Tall Poppies," *Art & Text*, January 1984, p. 52

Art Gallery of New South Wales, Sydney, *Australian Perspecta 1983: A biennial survey of contemporary Australian art*, May 12-June 26, 1983. Catalogue with text by Bernice Murphy and Janet Parfenovics

Artspace, Sydney, *Artists Books*, June 1983

Institute of Modern Art, Brisbane, *Minimalism x Six*, June-July 1983

Art Projects, Melbourne, *Robert MacPherson, Jenny Watson, Mike Parr, John Nixon,* July 1983

Heide Park and Art Gallery, Melbourne, *Australian Perspecta: Works on Paper,* opened July 1983. Traveled in Australia

Australian National Gallery, Canberra, *A Melbourne Mood: Cool Contemporary Art,* July-August 1983. Catalogue with text by Daniel Thomas

George Paton Gallery, University of Melbourne, *The End of Civilisation, Part II: Love Among the Ruins*, July-August 1983. Catalogue with text by Vivienne Shark LeWitt

Glasshouse Cinema, Royal Melbourne Institute of Technology, STUFF Concert 2, August 31, 1983

Galerie Biederberg-Mueller and Galerie Wetering, Amsterdam, *Australian Art in Amsterdam*, October 1983

ARC/Musée d'Art Moderne de la Ville de Paris, *D'un autre continent: l'Australie. Le rêve et le réel*, October 4-December 4, 1983. Catalogue with texts by Suzanne Pagé and Léon Paroissien

Art Projects, Melbourne, *Drawings (Schematic, Expressionist & Psychological),* December 1983

Art Gallery of South Australia, Adelaide, *Recent Australian Painting: A Survey 1970-1983*, December 1983-February 1984. Catalogue with text by Ron Radford

Art Projects, Melbourne, *Group*, April-May 1984

Roslyn Oxley9, Sydney, *Dreams and Nightmares*, April-May 1984

Los Angeles Institute of Contemporary Art, *Australia: Nine Contemporary Artists*, June-July 1984. Catalogue with text by Bob Smith and statement by the artist

Selected One-Man Exhibitions

Pinacotheca, Melbourne, June-July 1973; June 1974; August 1975; April 1977

Experimental Art Foundation, Adelaide, October 1975

Watters Gallery, Sydney, June 1976; April 1979

National Gallery of Victoria, Melbourne (with Peter Kennedy), October 1976

Barry Barker Ltd, London, July 1978; February 1980

Art Projects, Melbourne, February, September 1979; March, October 1980; (with Imants Tillers) July 31, 1982; April 1983; February 1984

Institute of Modern Art, Brisbane, April 1979

Art Projects Annex Program, Melbourne, April-May, July-August, November 1979

Institute of Temporary Art, Melbourne (two exhibitions), June-December 1979

Experimental Art Foundation, Adelaide, September 1979

Q Space, Brisbane, installations, February 4, March 14, 17, April 11, 14, May 6, 19, June 19, July 21, (with Robert MacPherson) September 1-5, 1980

Q Space Annex, Brisbane, installations, March 15, 29, April 12, 19, May 3, 10, 17, June 7, 14, 21, July 16, 17, 22, August 11, 12, September 5, 8, 12, November 25, 28, December 11, 1980; (with Robert MacPherson) April 3, 1981

V Space, Melbourne, installations, October 1980 (with Robert MacPherson); August 1, October 11, 1982; April-June, August 5, October 15, November 25, 1983

Q.E.D., Sydney, installation (with Imants Tillers), September 25, 1982

Yuhill/Crowley, Sydney, installation (with Imants Tillers), December 1982

Roslyn Oxley9, Sydney, February 1983

Roslyn Oxley9, Sydney, *John Nixon/Self Portrait/(Non-Objective Composition)*, July-August 1983. Catalogue with texts by Paul Taylor and the artist

Selected Bibliography

By the Artist

n-space, Sydney, 1980

"Manifesto for a Renewed Art Practice," *Art & Text*, no. 2, 1981

John Nixon Catalog Raisonné 1968-1981, Melbourne, 1981

John Nixon: Art Into Function/Production Prototype Models, Melbourne, 1982

Notes on Art Practice, Melbourne, 1982

"John Nixon/Imants Tillers," *Press*, June 1983

Of Blood and Hope, Melbourne, 1983

with Imants Tillers, *One Painting with Many Titles*, Melbourne, 1983

Scars of the Poet, Melbourne, 1983

Under the Veil of Darkness, Melbourne, 1983

"Young Blood" in *Notes on Art Practice*, Melbourne, 1983

On the Artist

Paul Taylor, "Angst in My Pants," *Art & Text*, September 1982, pp. 48-60

Stuff, February 1983

Press, March 1983

Sue Cramer, "Masterpieces and Tall Poppies," *Art Network*, vol. 10, June 1983, pp. 42-45

"John Nixon/Imants Tillers," *Press*, June 1983

Tension, August 1983

Robert Rooney, "Tall Poppies," *Flash Art*, November 1983, p. 74

Jill Montgomery, "AUSTRALIA—The French Discovery of 1983," *Art & Text*, January 1984, pp. 3-15

Jenny Watson, "Urgent Images," *Art & Text*, Winter 1984, p. 71

39 | *Self Portrait (Non-Objective Composition).*
1981-84
Artist's storeroom
Courtesy Art Projects, Melbourne

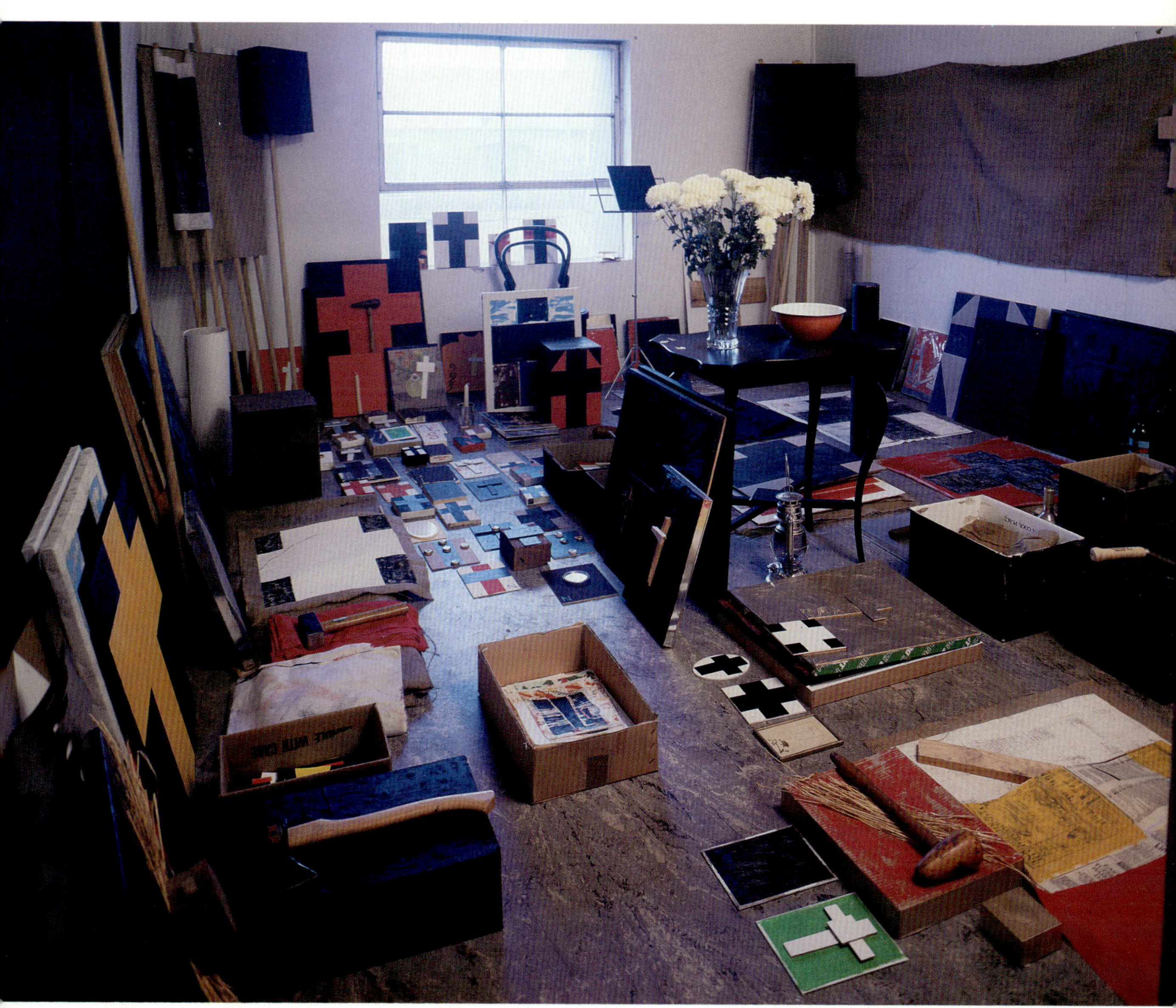

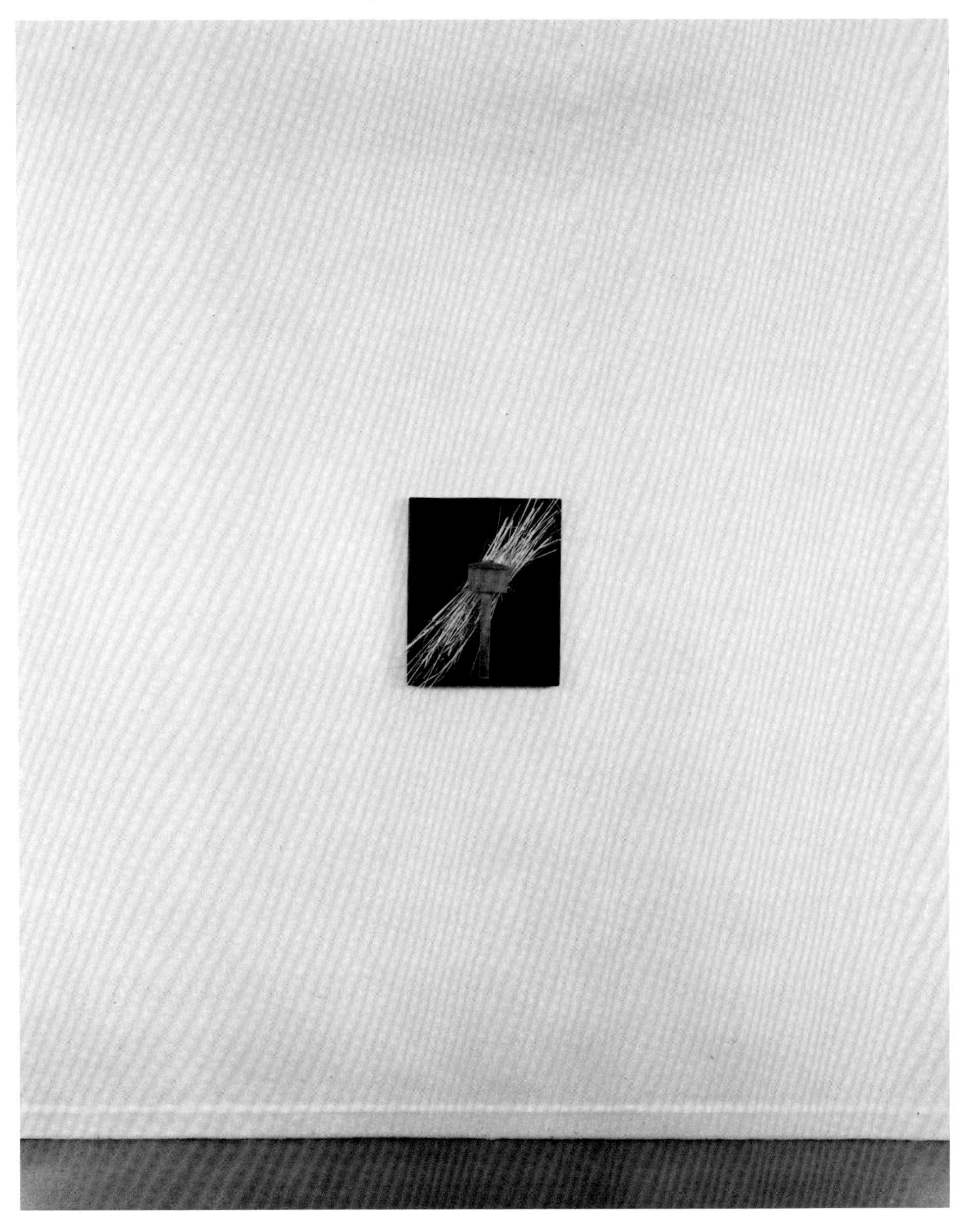

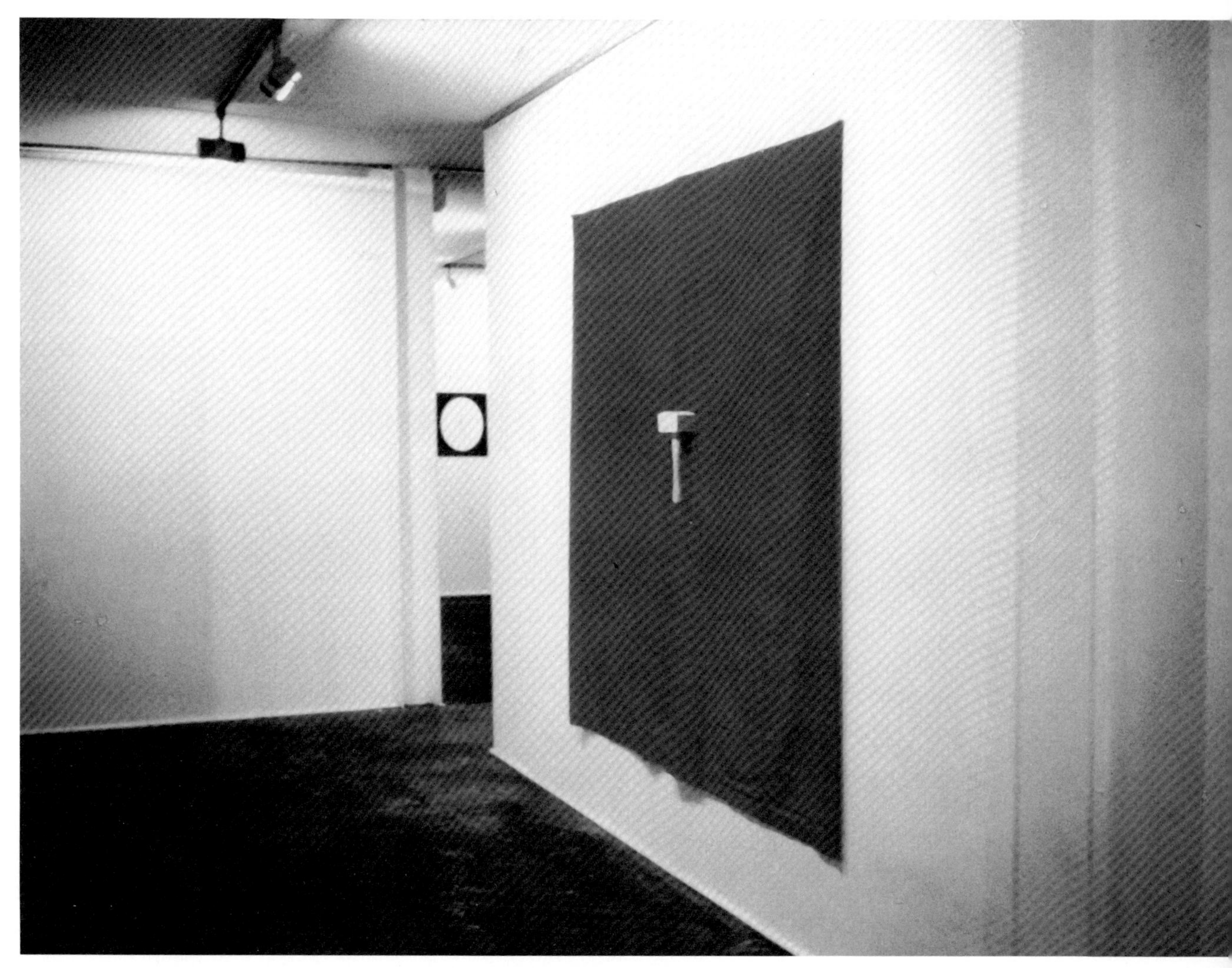

41 | Installation, Roslyn Oxley9, Sydney, July 1983

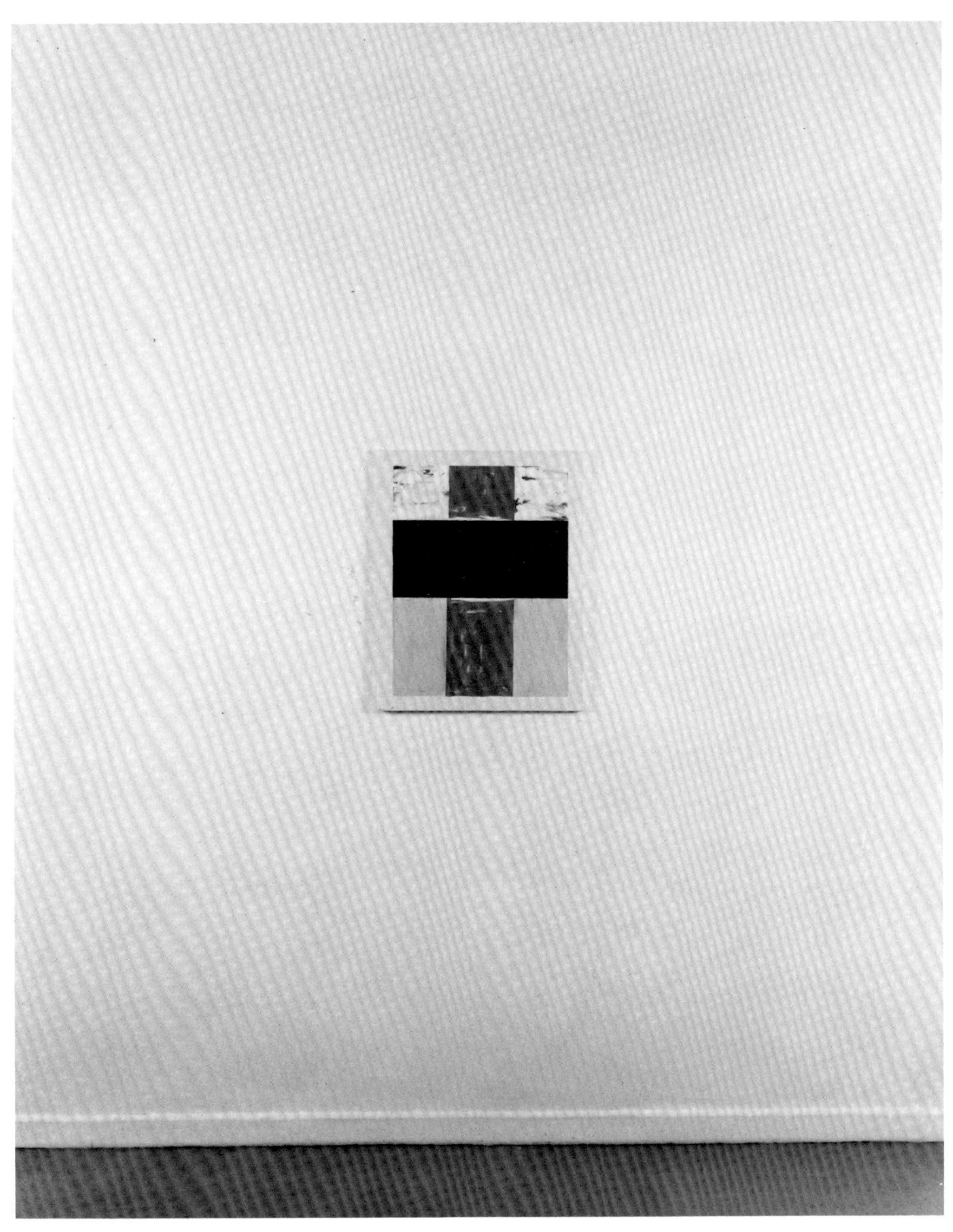

42 | *Self Portrait (Non-Objective Composition).* 1983
Acrylic on canvas, 24 x 20″ (61 x 51 cm.)
Courtesy Art Projects, Melbourne

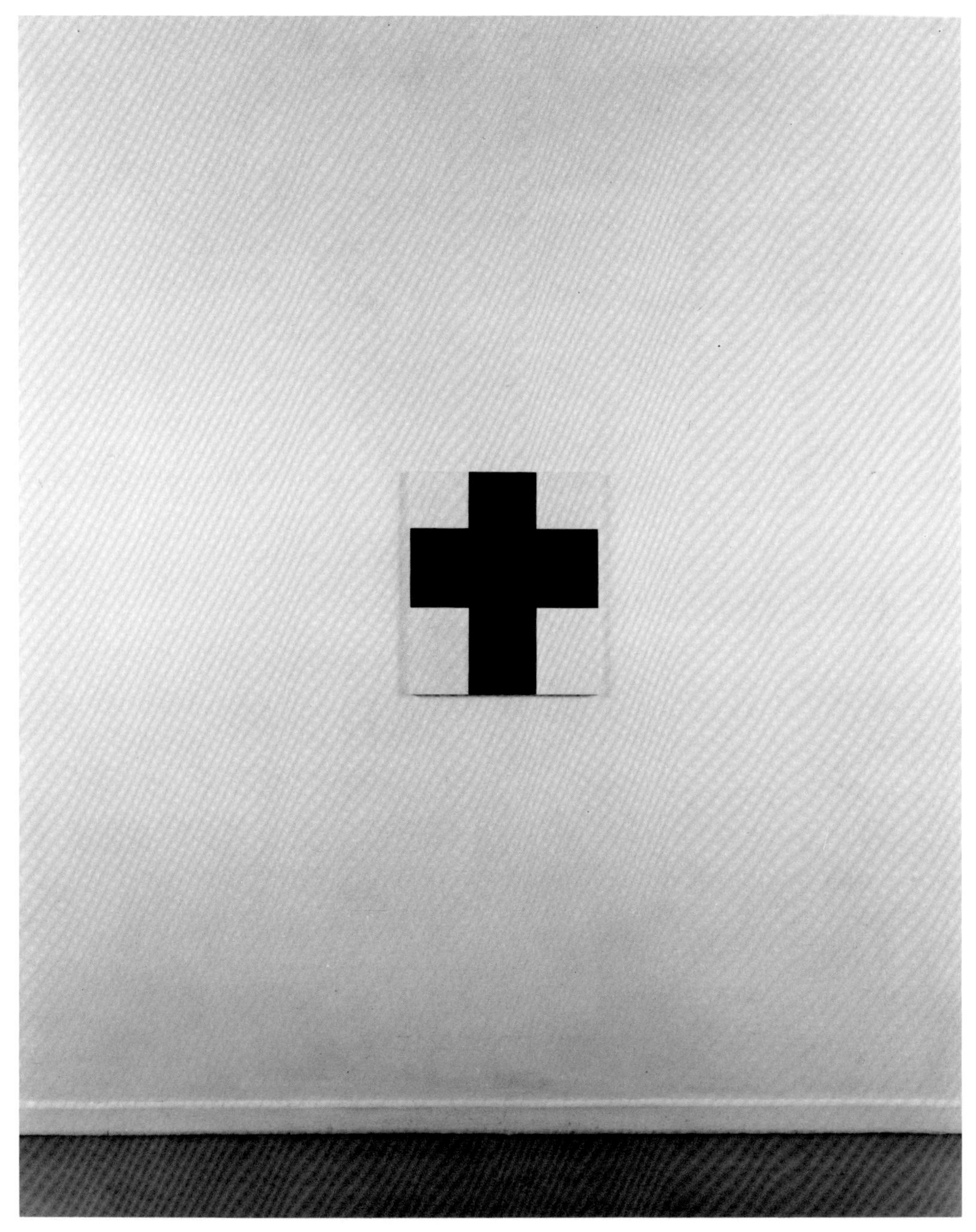

43 | *Self Portrait (Non-Objective Composition).* 1983
Oil and acrylic on canvas, 28 x 21⅝″ (71 x 55 cm.)
Courtesy Art Projects, Melbourne

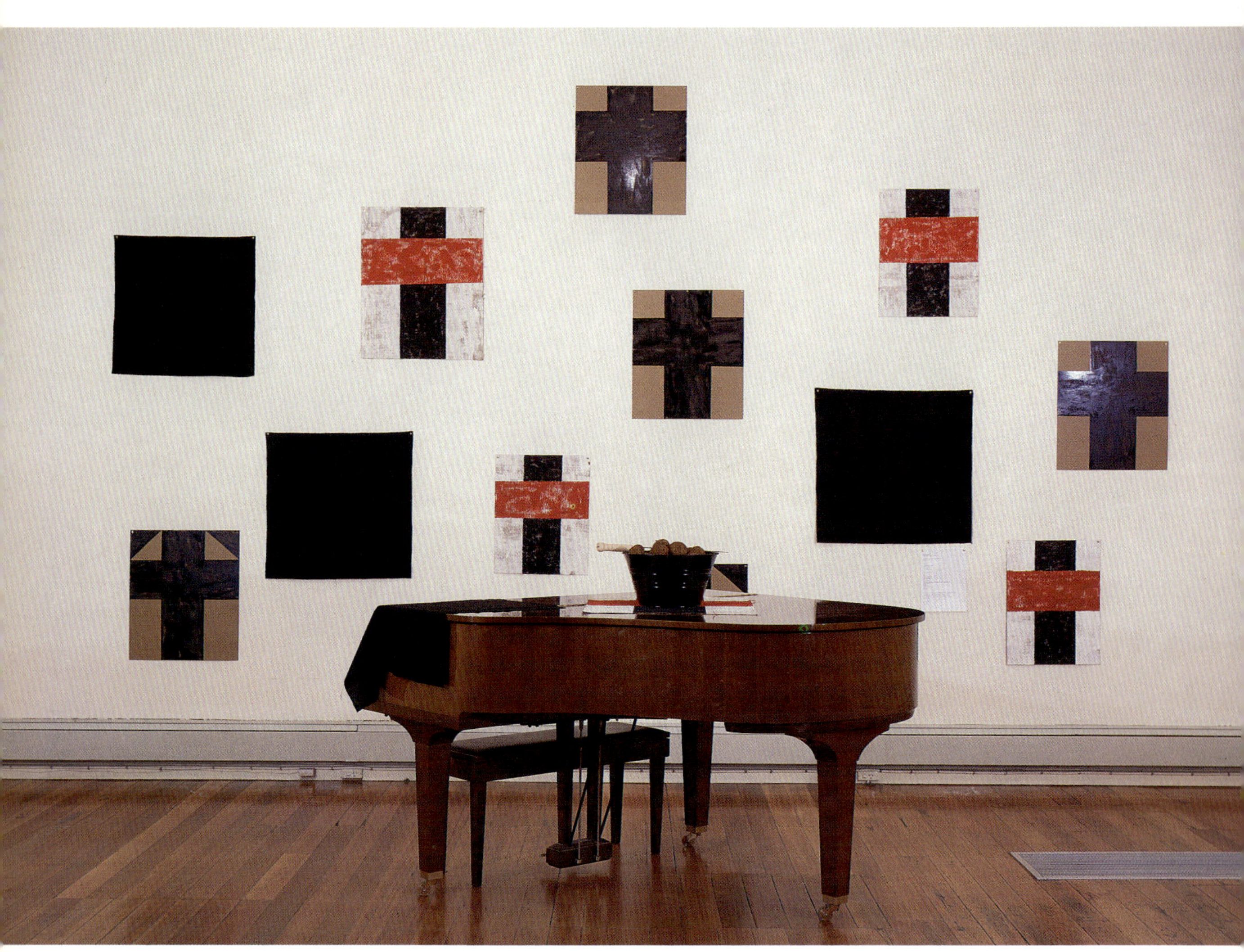

44 | *Self Portrait (Non-Objective Composition).* 1983
Installation, *Tall Poppies*, University Gallery,
University of Melbourne

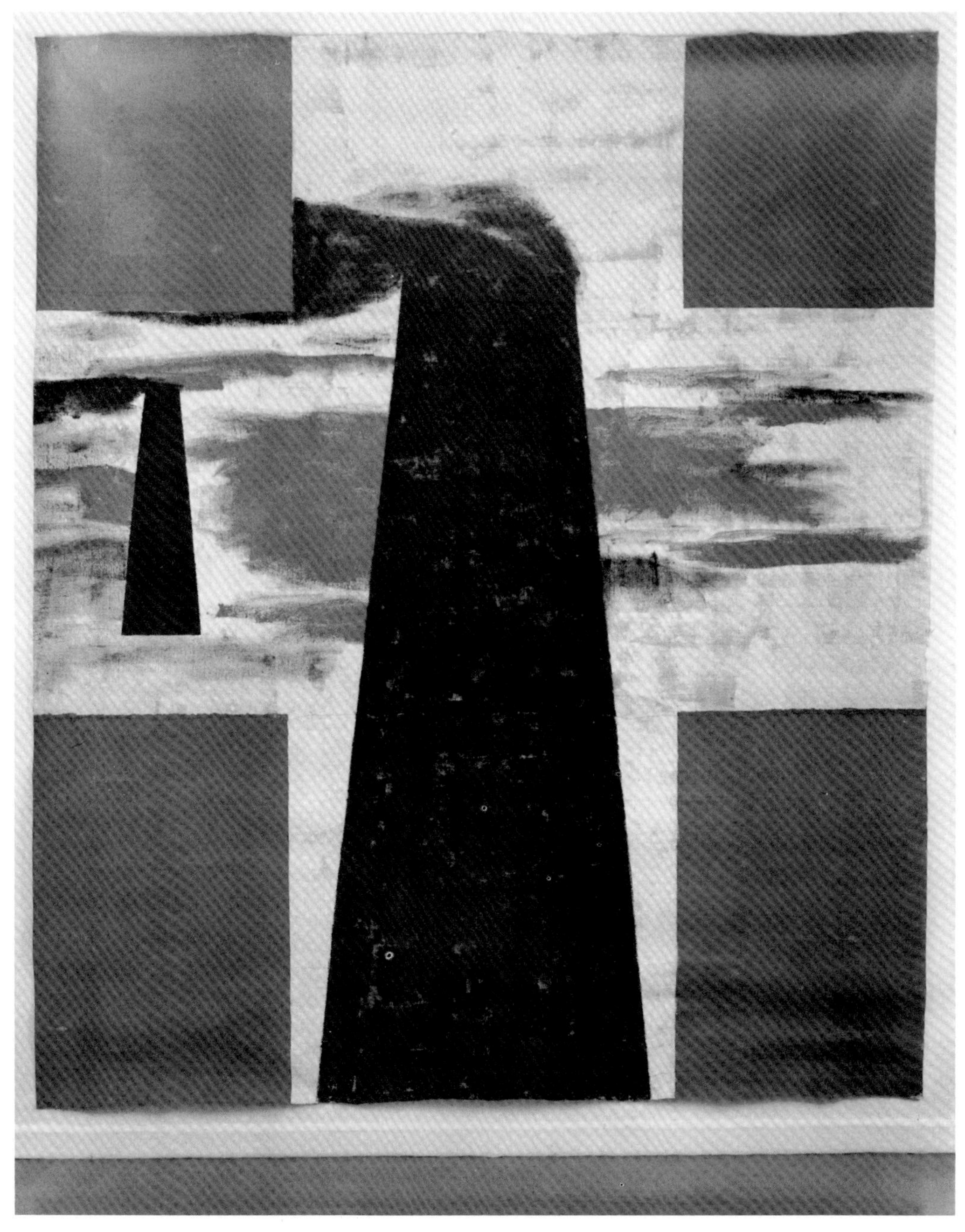

45   *Self Portrait (Architectonic Composition).* 1984
Acrylic on burlap, 113⅜ x 95¼″ (288 x 242 cm.)
Courtesy Art Projects, Melbourne

SUSAN NORRIE

Born in Sydney, 1953

National Art School, East Sydney Technical College, 1973

Victorian College of the Arts, Melbourne, Diploma of Painting, 1974-76

Travels in Europe, Japan and Egypt, 1977-78

Produces hand-painted T-shirts, 1979-84

Member of Artworkers Union (NSW)

Sydney Heritage Award, 1983

Part-time tutor of painting, Sydney College of the Arts, 1983

Artist in Residence, University Gallery, University of Melbourne, February-August 1984

Part-time tutor of painting, Victorian College of the Arts, Melbourne, 1984

Lives in Sydney

Selected Group Exhibitions

Students' Gallery (now Mori Gallery), Sydney, *Group Show*, July, December 1979

Art Gallery of New South Wales, Sydney, *Project 33: Artclothes*, December 1980-February 1981

Wollongong City Gallery, Wollongong, *New South Wales Young Contemporaries*, opened March 1981. Traveled in Australia until June 1981

Axiom Gallery, Melbourne, *Six Young Artists*, February 1982

Mori Gallery, Sydney, *Group Show*, December 1982

Commonwealth Bank, Sydney, *The Sydney Morning Herald Prize*, February 1983

Art Gallery of New South Wales, Sydney, *Australian Perspecta 1983: A biennial survey of contemporary Australian art*, May 12-June 26, 1983. Catalogue with text by Bernice Murphy and Janet Parfenovics

Ivan Dougherty Gallery, Sydney, *Attitude to Drawing*, July 1983

Mori Gallery, Sydney, *T-Shirt Show*, November 1983

Art Gallery of Western Australia, Perth, *Form ⟶Image ⟵ Sign: Biannual Survey of Contemporary Australian Art No. 3*, February-March 1984. Catalogue with text by Tony Bond

Selected One-Woman Exhibitions

Students' Gallery (now Mori Gallery), Sydney, August 1980

Mori Gallery, Sydney, July 1982

Realities, Melbourne, September 1983

Selected Bibliography

By the Artist

"Australia's Young Painters," *Vogue Living*, April-May 1981, p. 76

On the Artist

Mervyn Horton, "Exhibition Commentary," *Art and Australia*, vol. 18, Summer 1980, p. 115

Robert Rooney, "Six Young Moderns from Sydney," *The Age*, February 24, 1982, p. 14

Susannah Short, "Susan Norrie Makes a Fleshy Feminist Statement," *The Sydney Morning Herald*, October 14, 1982, p.8

Terence Maloon, "A Woman Takes a Macabre Look at Mummy's Baubles," *The Sydney Morning Herald*, October 23, 1982

Suzanne Davies and Richard Dunn, "Grappling with Diversity: Australian Perspecta 1983," *Art Network*, June 1983, pp. 12-14

Memory Holloway, "A glimpse into a private world," *The Age*, September 14, 1983, p.4

Ronald Millar, "Norrie turns out visual poetry," *The Herald,* September 15, 1983, p. 12

Suzanne Davies, "Susan Norrie—Realities," *Art Network*, September 1983, p. 51

Alan Krell, "Australian Perspecta '83," *Art and Australia*, vol. 121, September 1983, p. 168

Anne Dagbert, "Australian perspecta," *Art Press*, October 1983, p. 31

Elizabeth Butel, "The Rising Stars of '84," *The National Times,* December 30, 1983, p. 15

Terence Maloon, "Some Aspects of Art in Sydney, 1982," *Australian Art Review,* 1983, pp. 18-20

Bill Wright, "Australian Perspecta," *Studio International,* vol. 196, no. 1002, 1983, p. 20

Ursula Prunster, "Susan Norrie: Recent Works," *New York Art Express Magazine* (Australian issue), forthcoming in 1984

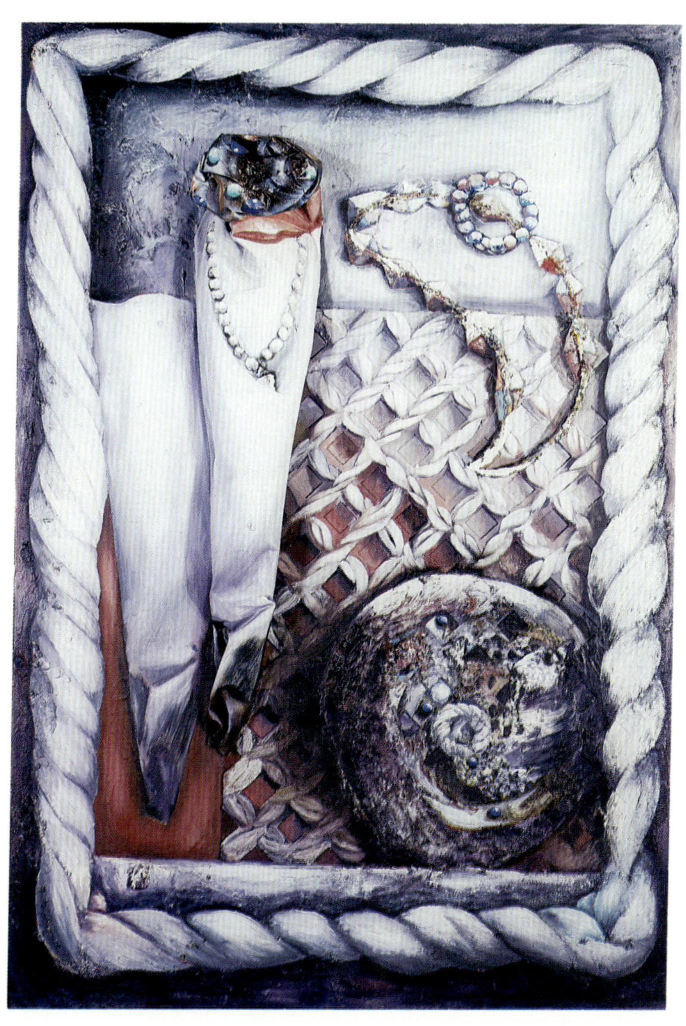

46 | *Suspended.* 1982
Mixed media and oil on plywood, 72 x 48″
(183 x 122 cm.)
Collection Art Gallery of Western Australia, Perth

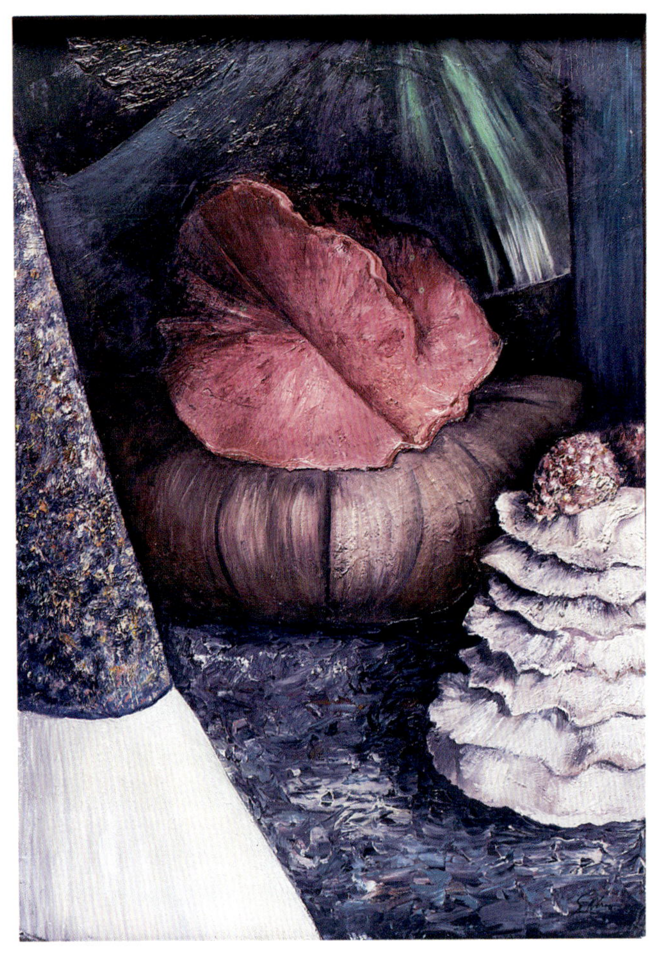

47 | *Wallflower.* 1983
Oil on board, 41¾ x 28⅞″ (105.9 x 73.3 cm.)
Private collection

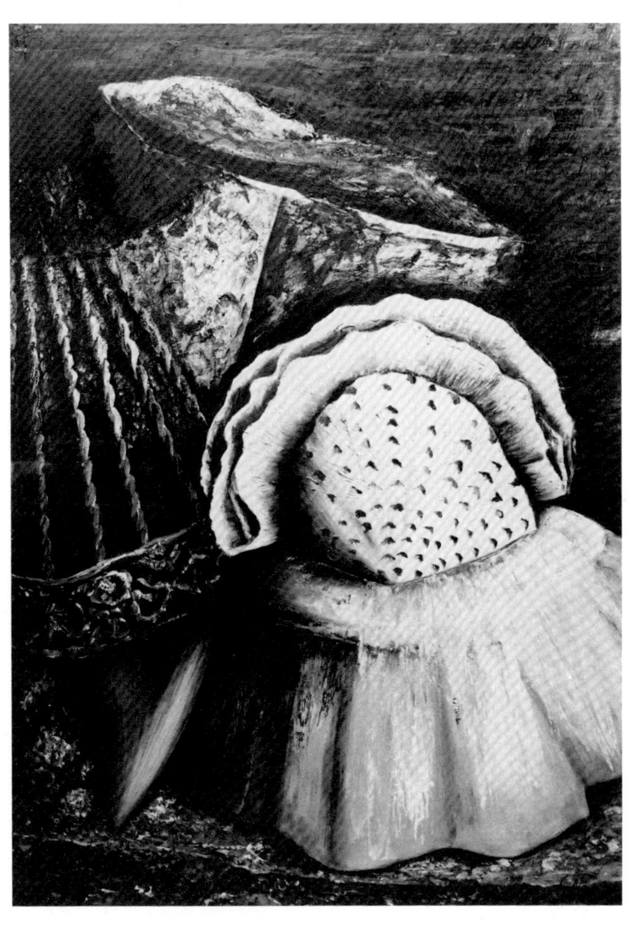

48 | *Charade.* 1983
Oil on board, 46½ x 33½" (118 x 85 cm.)
Private collection

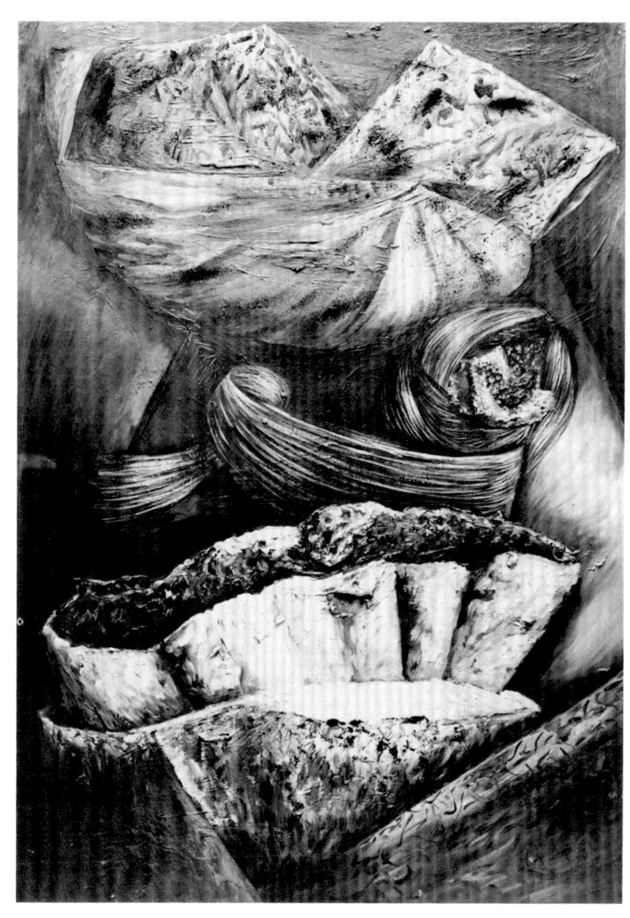

49 *Enshrouded.* 1983
Oil on board, 46½ x 33½″ (118 x 85 cm.)
Private collection

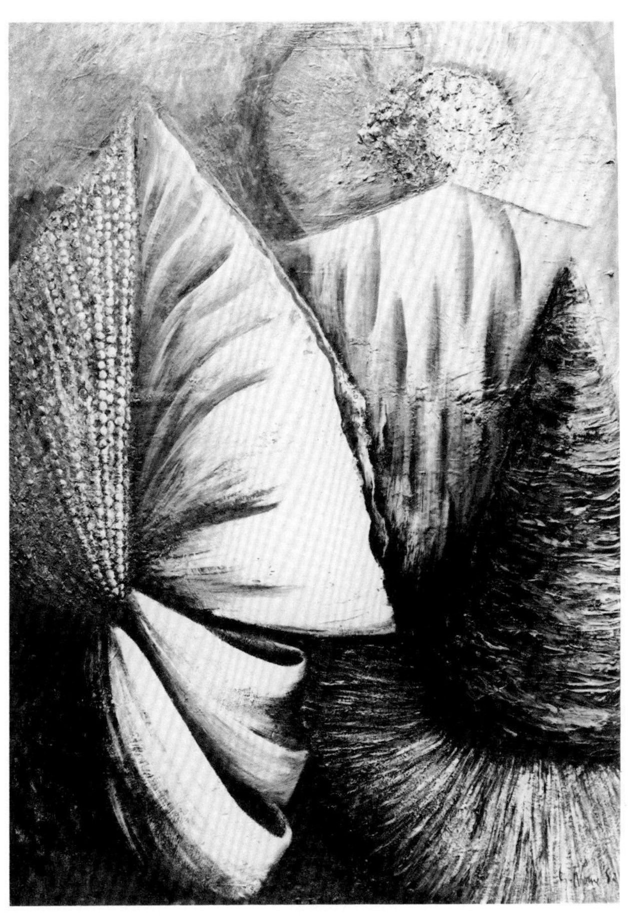

50 | *After the Dance.* 1983
Oil on board, 39 x 26⅜″ (99 x 67 cm.)
Collection Evi Robinson

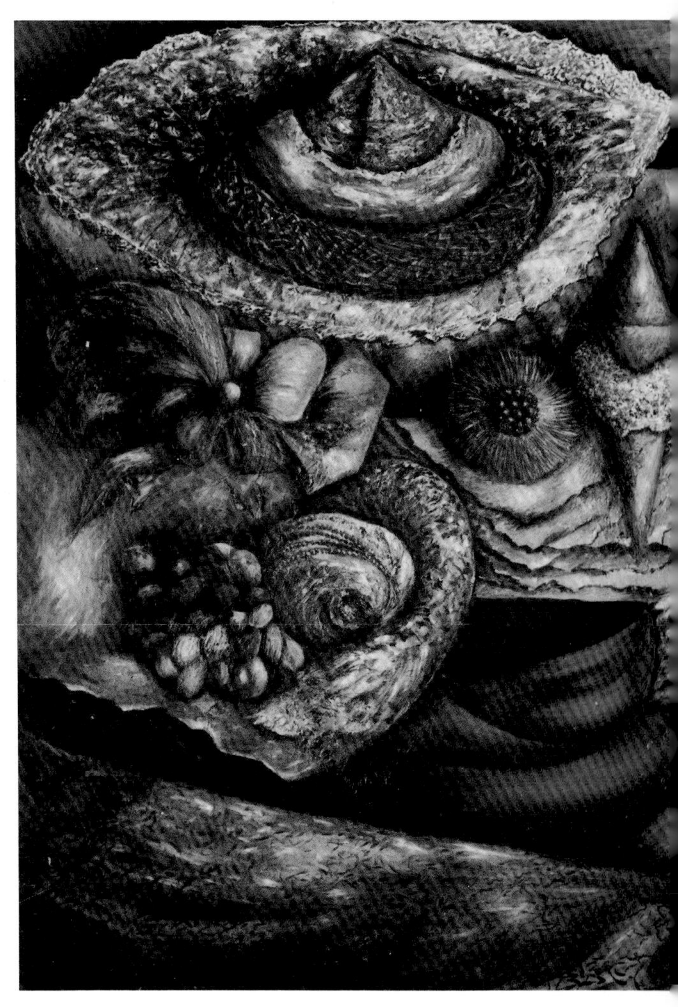

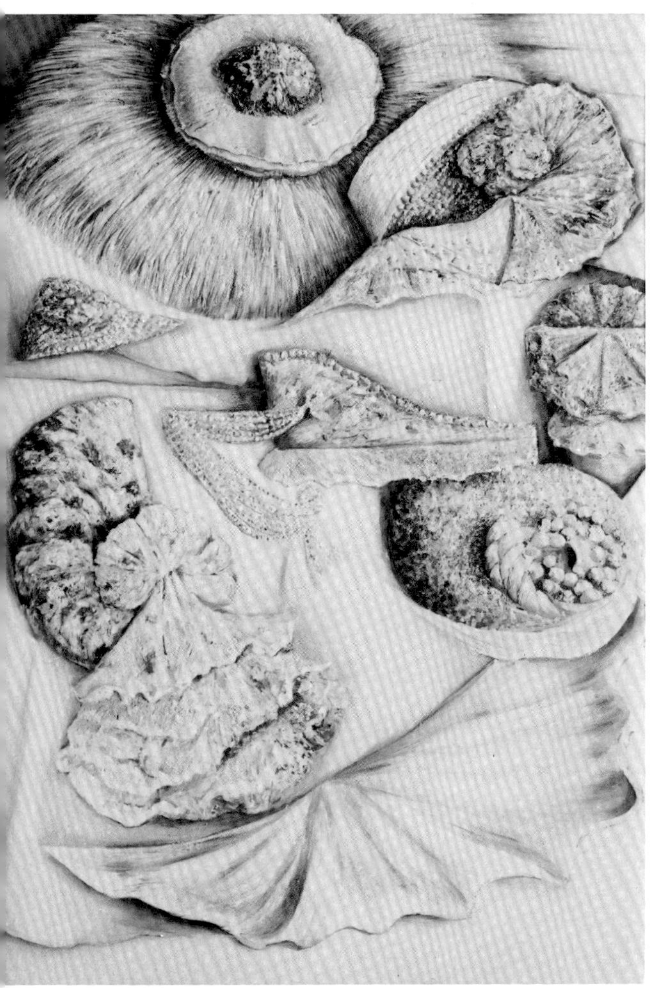 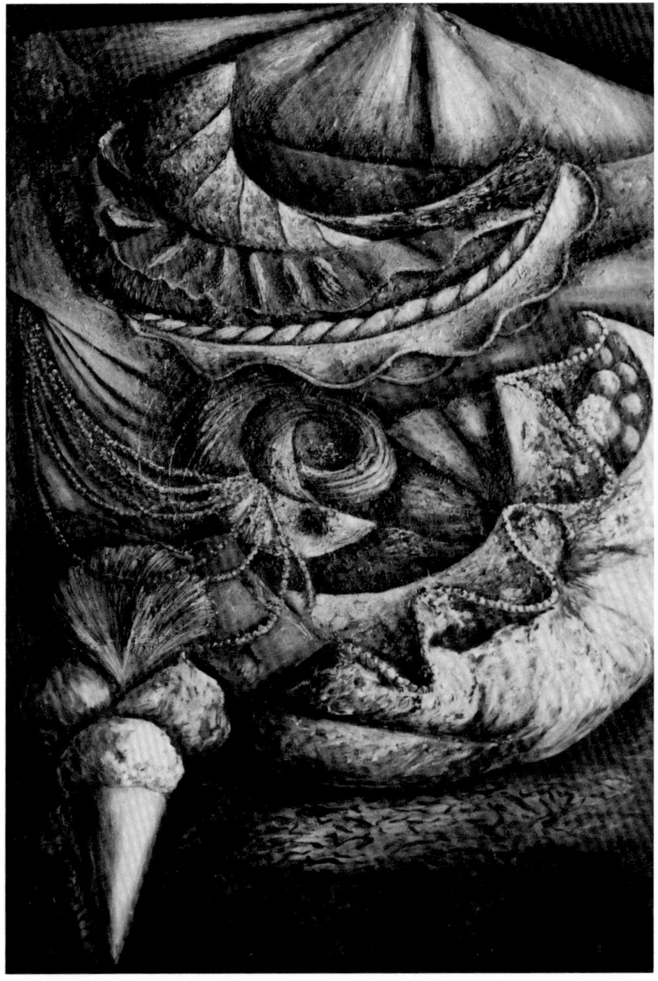

51 | *Triptych: I Fruitful Corsage; II Bridal Bouquet;*
III Lingering Veils. 1983
Oil on canvas, three panels, each 72 x 48″
(182.9 x 121.9 cm.)
Collection Art Gallery of New South Wales,
Sydney; Henry Salkauskas Contemporary Art
Purchase Fund, 1983

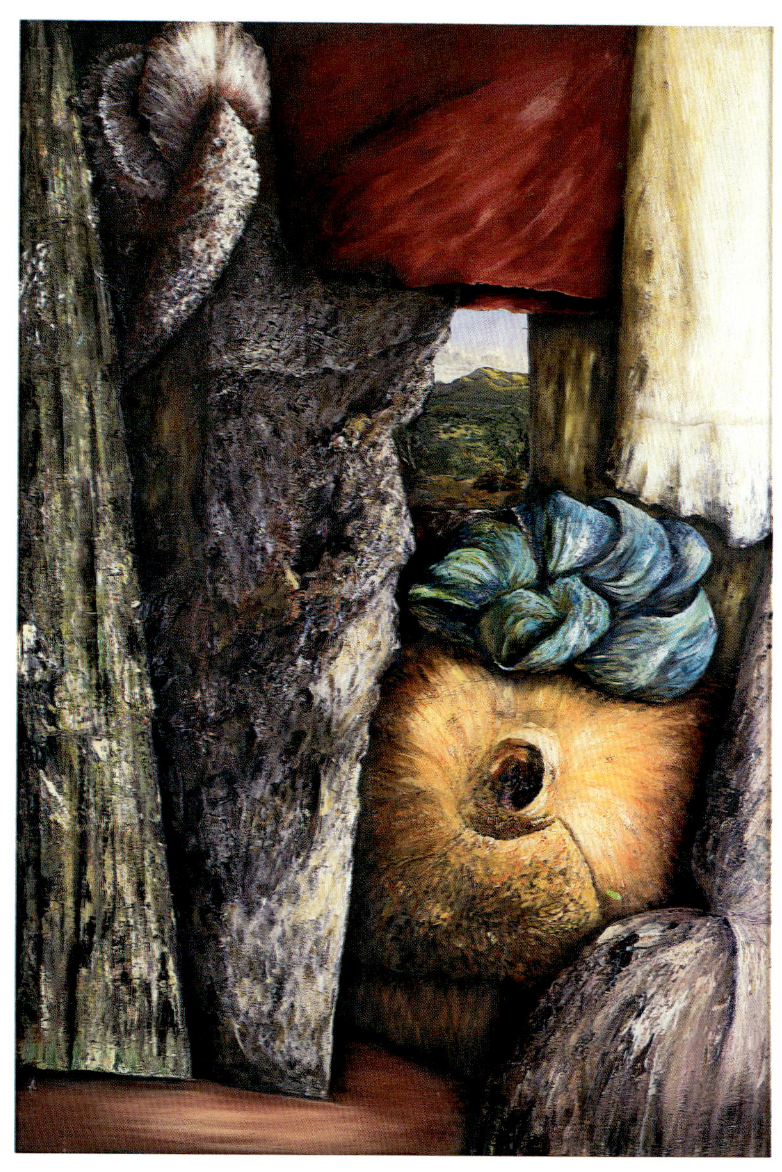

52 | *Lavished Living.* 1983-84
Oil on plywood, 72 x 48½″ (183 x 123 cm.)
Private collection

VIVIENNE SHARK LEWITT

Born in Sale, Victoria, 1956

Lives in Woomera, South Australia; Ipswich, Queensland; Perth; Pinang, Malaysia; Melbourne; Adelaide, 1956-76

Tasmanian School of Art, Hobart, 1976-79

Alexander Mackie College of Advanced Education, Sydney, 1980-81

Assistant Director, George Paton Gallery, University of Melbourne, 1982-84

Visual Arts Board Travel Grant, 1983

Lives in Melbourne

Selected Group Exhibitions

George Paton Gallery, University of Melbourne, *Artists' Books*, opened September 1978. Traveled in Australia and United States

Roslyn Oxley9, Sydney, *New Painting*, May-June 1982

Roslyn Oxley9, Sydney, *Pirates & Mutineers*, May 1983

Art Gallery of New South Wales, Sydney, *Australian Perspecta 1983: A biennial survey of contemporary Australian art*, May 12-June 26, 1983. Catalogue with texts by Bernice Murphy and Janet Parfenovics

George Paton Gallery, University of Melbourne, *The End of Civilisation, Part II: Love Among the Ruins,* July-August 1983. Catalogue with text by the artist; portion reprinted as "The End of Civilisation, Part II: Love Among the Ruins," *Art & Text,* no. 10, 1983, pp. 1-7

ARC/Musée d'Art Moderne de la Ville de Paris, *D'un autre continent: l'Australie. Le rêve et le réel*, October 4-December 4, 1983. Catalogue with texts by Suzanne Pagé and Léon Paroissien

Ballarat Fine Art Gallery, Victoria, *Animal Imagery in Contemporary Art*, December 1983-January 1984. Traveled to Wollongong Art Gallery, Wollongong, February

Selected One-Woman Exhibitions

Memorial Gallery of Fine Arts, University of Sydney, December 1981

Roslyn Oxley9, Sydney, May 1984

Selected Bibliography

By the Artist

"So this is real life...the continuing dissensions of New Wave Music," *The Tasmanian Review*, June 1979, p. 4

"Sur-Texts, Texts, Sub-Texts (Spot the Differences)," *R.A.T.*, May-June 1981

"Record Review," *Island Magazine*, June 1981, p. 5

"V.A.B. Project Survey," *Art Network*, June-November 1981, pp. 67-69

"Art and Video. The Birth of a Monster," *Brouhada*, no. 2, 1982

"Blitz? Who me?," *Bite Bite*, no. 1, 1982

"Tattslotto," *Stuff*, February 1983

"In the Desert," *Stuff*, August 1983

On the Artist

Paul Taylor, "Australian 'New Wave' and the 'Second Degree,' " *Art & Text*, April 1981, p. 32

Sandra McGrath, "Arts," *The Australian*, June 5-6, 1982, p. 11

Bernice Murphy, "Recent Painting in Australia," *Flash Art*, January 1983, pp. 56-59

Suzanne Davies and Richard Dunn, "Grappling with Diversity: Australian Perspecta 1983," *Art Network*, June 1983, p. 12

Anne Dagbert, "Australian perspecta," *Art Press*, October 1983, p. 31

Memory Holloway, "Art Journals: Progeny of the 1970s," *Australian Art Review*, October 1983, pp. 152-153

Interview with Robin Barden, "The End of Civilisation, Part II: Love Among the Ruins," *Tension*, no. 2, 1983, p. 5

Achille Bonito Oliva, "Recent Painting in Australia," *The International Trans-avantgarde*, January 1984, pp. 275-282

Jenny Watson, "Urgent Images," *Art & Text*, Winter 1984, p. 73

Bernice Murphy, "Some Recent Painting in Australia," *The International Trans-avantgarde*, 1984, pp. 275, 282

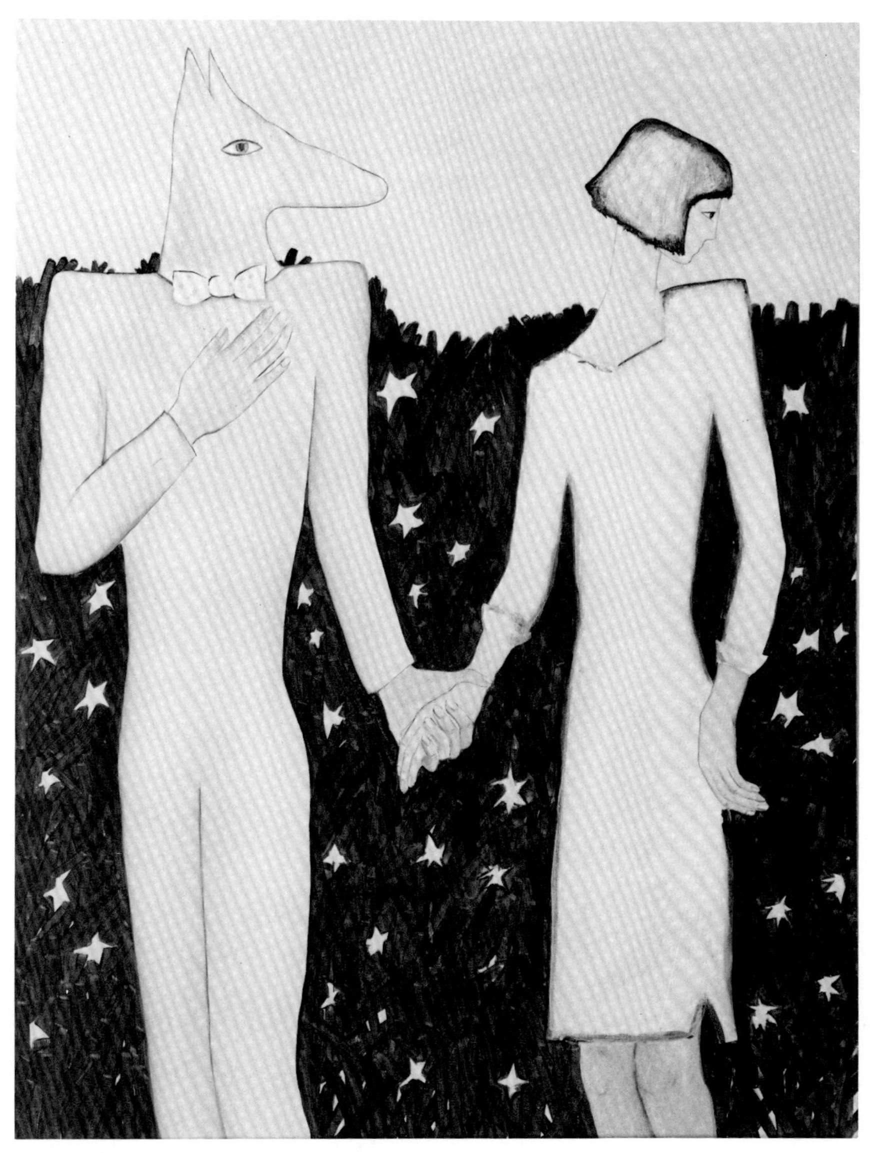

53 | *Anubis Marries (Another Time Another Place).*
1980
Acrylic on canvas, 47¼ x 35½″ (120 x 90 cm.)
Collection Mrs. E. Gregory

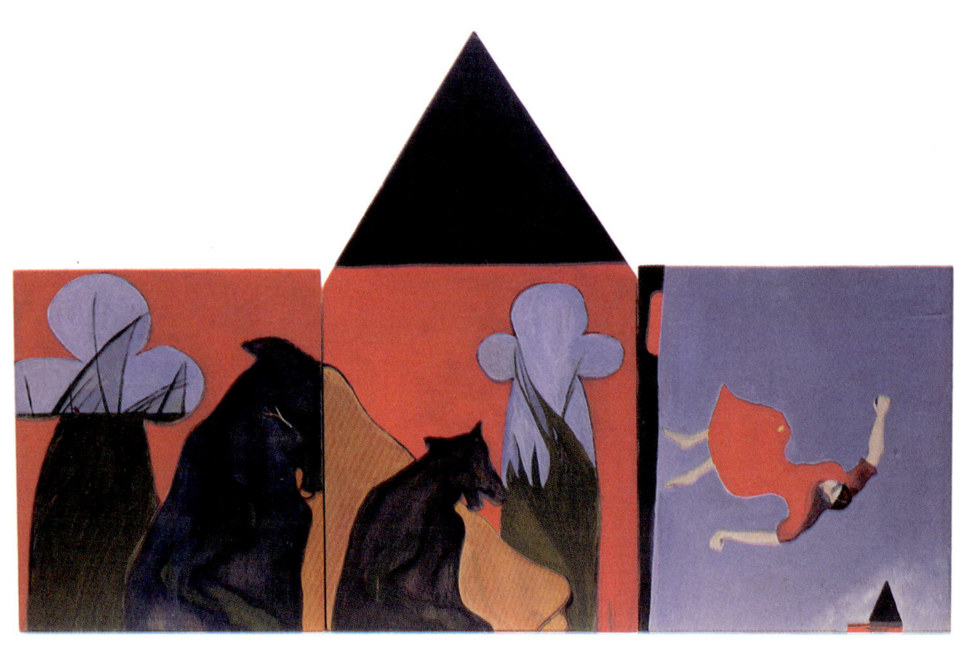

54 | *The Bloody Chamber.* 1983
Acrylic on wood, three panels, total 14½ x 22″
(37 x 56 cm.)
Collection University of Melbourne

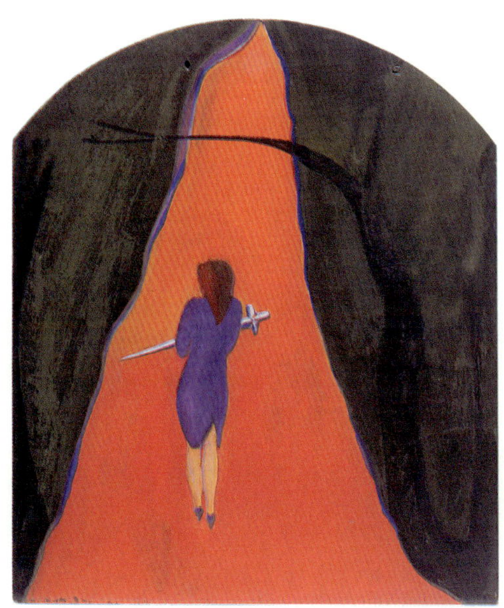 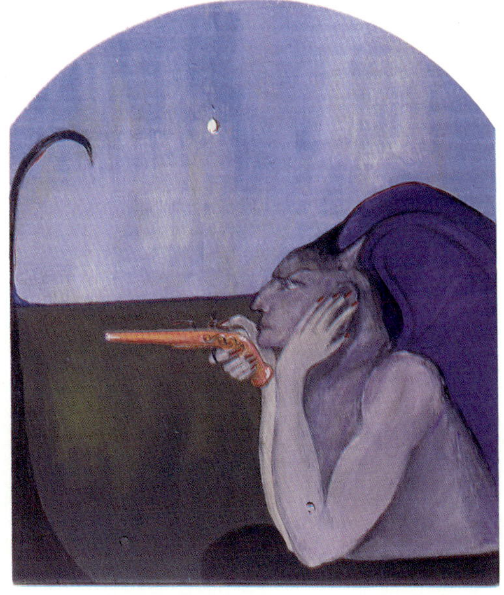

55 | *Charles Meryon the Voyeur. La Belle et la bête.*
1983
Acrylic on wood, two panels, total 13¾ x 23¾"
(35 x 60 cm.)
Collection Vivienne Sharpe

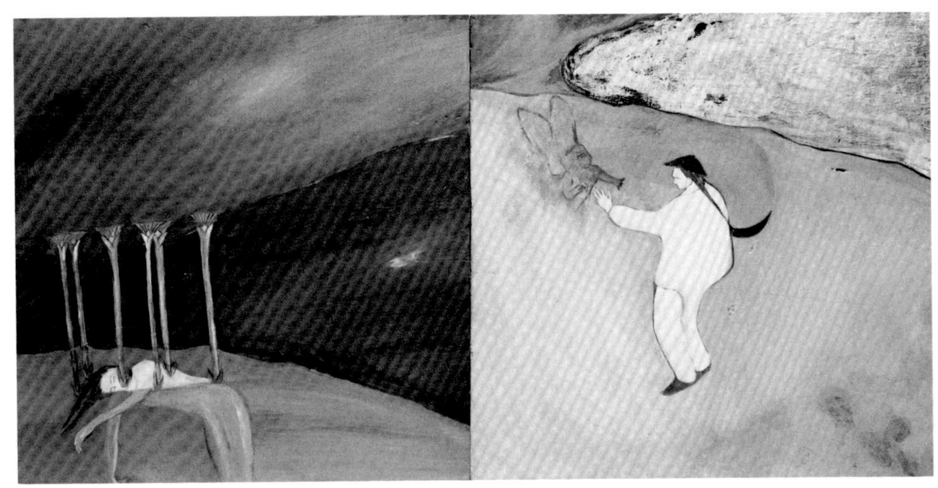

56 | *China Boy in the Desert. The Dead Girl.* 1983
Acrylic and gold leaf on wood, two panels, total
11 x 22″ (28 x 56 cm.)
Collection Naomi Cass

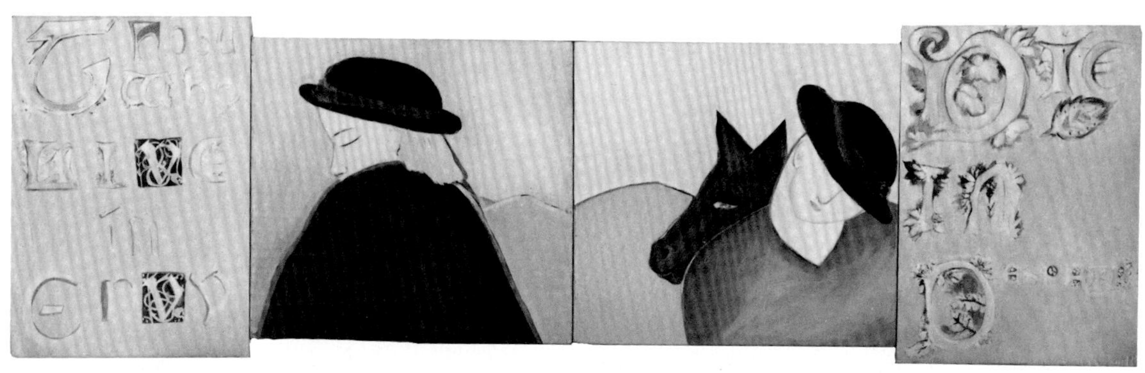

57 | *Those Who Live in Envy Die in Despair.* 1983
Acrylic on wood, four panels, total 10⅞ x 35″
(27.5 x 89 cm.)
Collection Louise Brentnall

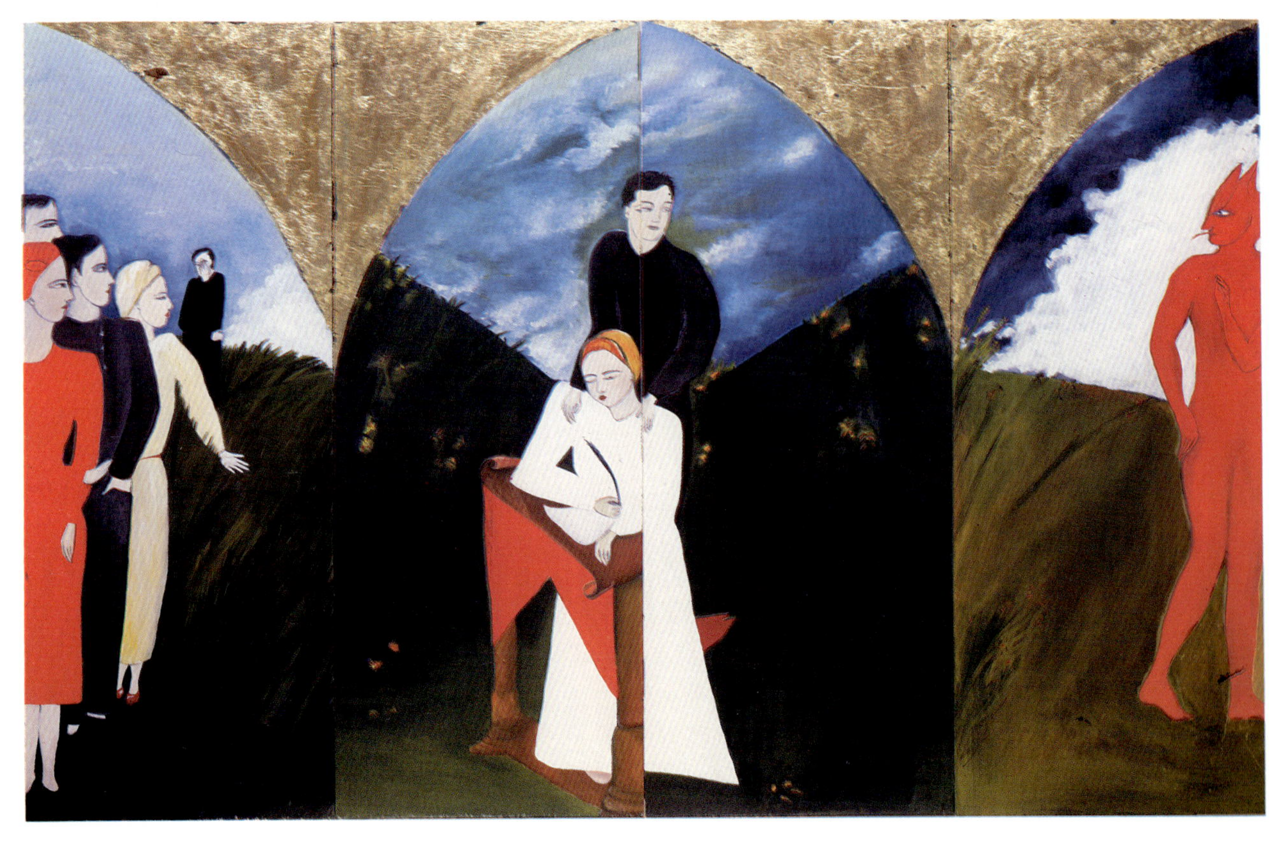

58 | *Goodness Always Triumphs over Evil.* 1984
Oil, gold leaf and acrylic on wood, four panels,
total 29½ x 45⅝″ (75 x 116 cm.)
Collection Janice and Greg Taylor

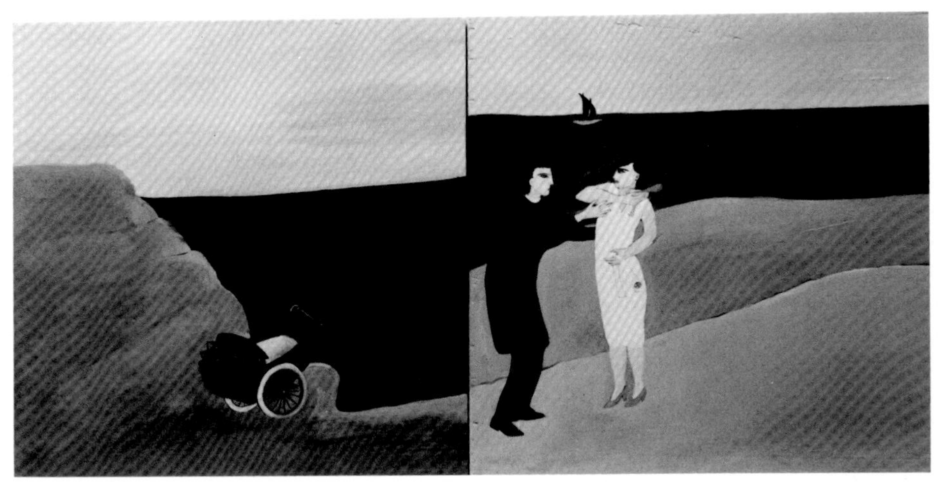

59 | *The Making of Leopold.* 1984
Acrylic on wood, two panels, total 11 x 22″
(28 x 56 cm.)
Courtesy Powell Street Gallery, Melbourne

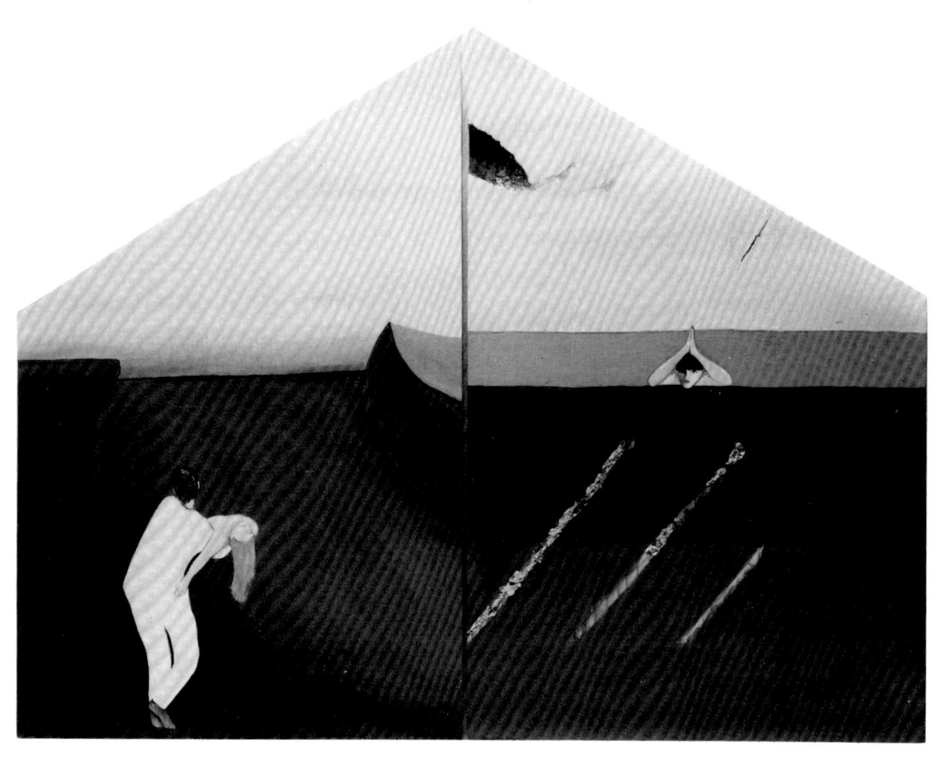

60 | *House of the True Heart* (unfinished). 1984
Acrylic on wood, two panels, total 18⅛ x 22″
(46 x 56 cm.)
Courtesy Roslyn Oxley9, Sydney

PHOTOGRAPHIC CREDITS

Color

Courtesy Art Gallery of Western Australia, Perth: cat. no. 46

Terence S. Bogue, Melbourne: cat. nos. 6, 7, 24, 39, 47, 54, 55, 58

Fenn Hinchcliffe, Sydney: cat. nos. 1, 3, 11, 13-15, 25, 28, 29, 36, 38, 52

Henry Jolles, Melbourne: cat. no. 32

Courtesy University Gallery, University of Melbourne: cat. no. 44

Black and White

Courtesy *The Age,* Melbourne: fig. 6

Courtesy Art Gallery of Western Australia, Perth: fig. 5

Terence S. Bogue, Melbourne: cat. nos. 4, 5, 8, 33, 37, 40, 42, 43, 45, 48-50, 56, 59, 60

From *Clotted Rot for Clots and Rotters,* Sydney: figs. 2, 3

Grant Hancock, Adelaide: cat. no. 10

Fenn Hinchcliffe, Sydney: cat. nos. 2, 12, 26, 27, 30, 31, 34, 35, 51, 53, 57

Henry Jolles, Melbourne: cat. no. 9

John Nixon, Melbourne: cat. no. 41

From *Punch,* Melbourne: fig. 7

Courtesy State Library of Victoria, Melbourne: fig. 1

From *Views in Australia:* fig. 4

Exhibition 84/7
6,000 copies of this catalogue, designed by
Malcolm Grear Designers and typeset by
Schooley Graphics, have been printed by
Eastern Press in September 1984 for the
Trustees of The Solomon R. Guggenheim
Foundation on the occasion of the exhibition
**Australian Visions: 1984 Exxon
International Exhibition.**